Paul Chamberlain

Talking about
GOOD
and
BAD
without getting
UGLY

A GUIDE TO
MORAL PERSUASION

IVP Books

An imprint of InterVarsity Press
Downers Grove, Illinois

InterVarsity Press
P.O. Box 1400, Downers Grove, IL 60515-1426
ivpress.com
email@ivpress.com

InterVarsity Press® is the book-publishing division of InterVarsity Christian Fellowship/USA®, a movement of students and faculty active on campus at hundreds of universities, colleges and schools of nursing in the United States of America, and a member movement of the International Fellowship of Evangelical Students. For information about local and regional activities, visit intervarsity.org.

Design: Cindy Kiple

Images: handshake: Digital Vision/Getty Images
        man's thumb: Photodisc Collection/Getty Images
        woman's thumb: Nick Koudis/Getty Images

ISBN 978-0-8308-3268-2

Printed in the United States of America ∞

Library of Congress Cataloging-in-Publication Data

Chamberlain, Paul, 1954-
    Talking about good and bad without getting ugly : a guide to moral
persuasion / by Paul Chamberlain.
        p. cm.
    Includes bibliographical references.
    ISBN 0-8308-3268-8 (alk. paper)
    1. Ethics. 2. Ethical problems. 3. Imaginary conversations. I.
Title.
    BJ1031.C493 2005
    170—dc22

                                                         2004025513

P   19   18   17   16   15   14   13   12   11   10   9   8   7   6   5   4   3   2

Y   31   30   29   28   27   26   25   24   23   22   21   20   19   18   17   16

To Tyler,

who made me a father and

since then has tested my ethical theories in more ways than one.

They are stronger because of you.

CONTENTS

1

TO ENGAGE OR
NOT TO ENGAGE

Risky Terrain Ahead

W hatever you do, do not bring up politics or religion if you want to maintain polite social company." I still remember receiving this bit of advice as a young person from someone who obviously thought I needed to hear it. *Why do I have to avoid them,* I wondered, *especially since they are among my favorite topics of discussion?*

Then one day I witnessed a conversation around our family dining table that shed light on the matter. We had two out-of-town guests that day who happened to be on opposite ends of the political spectrum and who were anything but bashful about letting others know where they stood. Early into the meal both guests confidently set forth their unsolicited political views and voting patterns, and announced to everyone at the table why they could never vote for the political party of the other guest. And we weren't even in the middle of an election campaign. What is more, these two political proponents were married to each other. Needless to say, what had up to that point been a happy and carefree social event immediately turned into a state of subdued warfare that never really disappeared until the guests were gone.

It is precisely to avoid situations like this one that we are commonly advised, for our own good, to steer clear of these hot topics. After all, who wants to destroy perfectly serene social events? Go ahead, goes the warning, have your views on politics and religion, believe them as strongly as you want to, but keep them to yourself in polite company. Otherwise you'll be sorry.

Soon after processing this piece of advice, however, I realized there was more to the story. Politics and religion are not the only topics that belong on the list (if we have one). Questions of *ethics* and *morality* can carry at least as much potential for wrecking a good party as politics or religion, and I discovered that a person could be just as sorry he or she had raised an ethical issue as one of politics or religion. These topics require great care, and that is not always demonstrated. We've all probably witnessed discussions of an ethical issue being handled in a boorish manner. Consider this way of introducing yourselves to the hostess as guests at a lavish party.

Hostess: Welcome, it's so nice to see you two. You both look positively dashing tonight! Your names are . . . ?

Guest: Hi. My name is John. This is my wife, Grace, and we believe stem-cell research using embryos should be banned—post haste!

Hostess (somewhat taken aback): Oh, I see . . . uh . . .

John: You do, do you? Then where has your opposition been to the bill now being debated in the legislature? I didn't see your name on the petition we sent around last week.

Hostess (desperately searching for words): Well, I guess issues like these are controversial, and besides, I think I was out shopping when the petition came around.

Grace (grabbing her coat): Out shopping? Controversial? A human life is controversial? Now I've heard everything! C'mon John, let's get out of here.

Hostess (breathing a sigh of relief as she watches the two guests disappear out the back door and whispering to herself): Well, thanks for coming, I think.

Clearly there are better ways than John and Grace's method of raising moral questions, but the fact remains that discussing good and evil in our culture can be a perilous undertaking. If we decide to proceed down this path, the way forward is fraught with potential pitfalls, and most of us have encountered some of them at one time or another. Questions such as stem-cell research, capital punishment, abortion, euthanasia, animal

> **DISCUSSING GOOD AND EVIL IN OUR CULTURE CAN BE A PERILOUS UNDERTAKING.**

rights, war and peace, and same-sex marriage are not only controversial, they are highly emotional for many people as well. They involve serious dynamics such as genuine suffering, personal autonomy, human rights (women's rights in particular) and the dignity and value of human life.

Nor do we always know the personal history or life experience of the person we are speaking to. For us to assert over the back fence that abortion is murder may be to condemn our neighbor of having murdered her own child. To confidently tell a room full of people that removing a patient from life-support is always wrong may be to send the message to someone in the room that he wrongly terminated his mother's life a few months ago. Likewise, to tell a soldier who has just returned from a tour of active duty that wartime killing is immoral may be to consign that soldier to the category of mass murderer.

No wonder many of us keep our distance from issues like these. The risks and frustrations are simply too great, and we have become gun shy. We've concluded that we can't win on this messy turf, so it's better to stay away from it altogether. Wading into it is akin to tiptoeing through a minefield with no guidebook to tell us where the mines are. Our attempts to talk about good and bad all too often turn downright ugly.

That brings us to the focus of this book, which is devoted precisely to helping us develop our skills in talking about issues of good and bad without getting ugly. I am convinced this can be done, and at the risk of sounding smug I say this as someone with special credentials in this area. Whether due to my own latent, masochistic tendencies or simply my own desire to spend a career working with the issues I've always wanted to talk about anyway, I ended up earning my final academic degree in three specific areas of specialization: *ethics, political* philosophy and philosophy of *religion.* Precisely the three hot-button issues we are regularly warned to steer clear of. Consequently I have spent the past eighteen years teaching, writing and talking about these issues with students, colleagues, debating opponents, friends and family members. My experience has taught me that positive, meaningful dialogue on the moral questions confronting our culture is not only *possible,* it's more *necessary* than ever. We must engage our culture on these important issues.

I say this for two reasons. First, engaging others is one of the best ways available to think through and hone our own positions on difficult moral questions. This is especially true if we are willing to go beyond our comfort zone and interact at least partly with those who don't see things our way. Allowing those on the other side of an issue to see and examine *our* moral perspectives through *their* glasses can be very revealing—they may see things we don't. Of course the benefit can be mutual because we may see things they don't. We will usually find that different views on any single issue are rooted in more fundamentally different ways of looking at life and the world. This has a way of leading our discussions into these deeper foundational issues.

It's wise to remember that our primary goal in thinking through moral issues is not to improve our skills at pointing out all that is wrong with others' moral views. Rather we seek moral truth in order to formulate wise and thoughtful positions we can live by. Correct living is greatly helped by correct moral knowledge.

Second, profitable discussion with others is our way of contributing to our culture as it struggles with new and complex moral issues. Seldom has there been greater interest in ethical questions. University ethics classes across North America are often full, requiring new sections to be added regularly. Ethics seminars are common, and ministers are frequently called on to advise parishioners on various ethical dilemmas they are facing. Can we make a contribution to our culture in its obvious cry for moral clarity and insight? I am convinced we can, and useful dialogue is the way to do so. The more thoughtful and well-reasoned our moral positions are, the greater our contribution will be.

My hope is that this book will be something of a map, or should I say an atlas, to help us talk about good and bad without getting ugly; a guide for engaging issues that so often leave us confused and exasperated. Following the map will mean developing certain skills all of us already possess and using these skills to greater benefit. We need to become adept at sorting out points of confusion, clarifying the messages we're bombarded with and asking the right questions about them. We also need to probe deeper and identify the assumptions and perspectives lurking behind these moral messages. To put it simply, we need to learn to think clearly and consistently about the moral issues facing us.

But confronting moral issues has become an increasingly complicated and thorny endeavor in this new millennium. New twists and turns have sprung up, changing the moral landscape considerably and creating a moral maze that is anything but simple to navigate. Long-held assumptions and traditions about good and evil and about life itself have been set aside with new ones taking their place.

At the same time, exploding technology has given us new capabilities that were unimaginable only a few decades ago. With these capabilities have come new and increasingly complex moral questions. Does the fact that we are *able* to do something automatically give us the *moral permission* to do it? Obviously not, since we all *can* do many things that we *should not* do. But then where are the ethical lines to be drawn? How can we know when we ought not do something that our technologies have enabled us to do? In short, how can we navigate our way through the new moral questions created by our ever-expanding technological capabilities? In the next two chapters I will address this changing moral landscape and the part technology has played in changing it.

But if technology has created new and perplexing dilemmas, it is the radically new moral messages bombarding our culture over the past few years that have made these dilemmas even more difficult to discuss, let alone resolve. "Morality is a personal and private matter, and you should keep it that way," we hear over and over again. "Your moral values are neither right nor wrong; they are merely expressions of *your* attitudes and belief systems. But our culture is pluralistic and multicultural, and other people have different moral values that you should also respect as expressions of *their* beliefs."

WE NEED TO LEARN TO THINK CLEARLY AND CONSISTENTLY ABOUT THE MORAL ISSUES FACING US.

How do we even get started engaging moral issues with people who think this way about morality? Doing so runs the risk of violating others' privacy. Furthermore, on this way of thinking, no moral viewpoint could ever be simply right or wrong anyway, so what would be the point of engaging others on these questions in the first place? What causes people to think this way about morality, especially people who appear to appreciate and commend good behavior and condemn bad conduct when they see it? In chapter two I will explore what lies behind these and other "new" moral messages so commonly heard in Western culture. In chapter three I will discuss the moral dilemmas presented by new technologies that raise new, previously unimagined possibilities. And in chapter four I will highlight and untangle some of the moral confusion resulting from our culture's attempts to address moral dilemmas with these prevailing attitudes.

In chapters five and six I will address two specific challenges encountered by anyone who has attempted to talk about good and bad: first, the demand to be *tolerant* of other people's views and values in our pluralistic age, and second, the claim that we have no right to *impose* our moral values on others. What do these statements mean, and how would we carry them out? Does tolerance require accepting all moral views as equally good regardless of what they approve or disapprove? If not, what then? And how exactly do we go about imposing our moral values onto others? These statements, while containing valuable insights, involve a bundle of confusion that I will attempt to untangle.

In chapter seven I will regroup and explicitly put on the table a number of key moral foundations, rock-solid ideas that can guide us through confusing times. That leaves the final chapter, where I will ask the most important question of all: How can we make a difference in our society? This is what it's all about. After all, interacting with others on the important moral and social issues of our day was never intended to be a purely academic pursuit. We have an opportunity to make real differences, sometimes life and death differences. It is hard to imagine many opportunities more worthy of capitalizing on than this one.

My hope is that as you join me on the trip, you will be challenged to become a more astute and active participant in the ongoing moral and social discussions swirling around us in our culture. These take place in legislatures, community halls, churches, newspaper editorial sections, restaurants, living rooms and over backyard fences across the world. We can engage others in discussion, whether formally or informally, and if this book encourages you to do even a little more of that, it will have fulfilled its purpose.

2

REDRAWING THE MAP

Our Changing Moral Landscape

We will rid the world of this evil!" The president's words were passionate and understandable. Days earlier, the World Trade Center and Pentagon had been attacked by terrorists who had hijacked commercial airliners and flown them, passengers and all, into these massive symbols of economic and military might. As he spoke, the twin towers of the World Trade Center lay collapsed in smoldering heaps of rubble on the ground, with thousands of innocent people buried beneath them, most of whom had nothing to do with the national policies that had provoked these attacks.

We all know exactly where we were and what we were doing when we heard the shocking news of this event that has now come to be referred to simply as 9/11. Besides the overwhelming terror and loss of life caused by the incoming airliners, huge amounts of property and equipment had been destroyed, the economy was reeling, and the nation, indeed the entire continent, was seething. It was all so sudden, so brutal, so horrifying. Even then it was being described as the worst act of terrorism the world had ever seen.

But I had to ask myself, could the president do it? Could he really rid the world not just of this evil but of any evil? Were we really counting on him to carry through on such a lofty pledge? If so, there were some foundational questions the people of our culture would need to ask, questions upon which there would be widespread disagreement.

KNOWING GOOD AND EVIL?

Consider the following conversation between Isaac, a new member of the university fraternity house, who is still functioning on traditional, "old," moral thinking, and Michael, a seasoned member, on the day following 9/11.

Michael: Good morning Isaac.

Isaac: I hope so!

Michael: You what?

Isaac: I hope it's a good morning, at least better than yesterday morning. What a horrible day that was!

Michael: Yes, that was totally unacceptable wasn't it. People should be able to find other ways of getting their point across.

Isaac: Now I've really seen evil. Pure, unadulterated evil.

Michael: It was disgusting, wasn't it. Highly inappropriate. Way out of line. But I'd be careful about using words like *evil* to describe it.

Isaac: Careful? Why careful? Haven't you watched the news? Thousands of people who were alive yesterday, just going about their business like any ordinary day, are lying dead beneath the World Trade Towers. They were murdered en masse. If there ever was a time when the word *evil* applied, this is it, wouldn't you agree?

Michael: I agree that this kind of thing shouldn't have happened.

Isaac: But you don't want to call it evil. What's up with that?

Michael: Actually, I'm not sure we should be using those stark moral terms, *good* and *evil,* anymore at all. There are just too many problems with them.

Isaac: What problems?

Michael: For starters, what is evil to you may be good to someone else. Didn't you see the news last night? And who are we to impose our ideas of good and evil on other people anyway?

Isaac: Yes, I saw the news and was disgusted by it. People voicing pleasure at airplanes full of people flying into the trade towers.

Michael: My point exactly. You think it is evil. They think it is good.

Isaac: Anyone who thinks this was good must be . . .

Michael: Hey, not so fast! Not only do they think it was good, they're thanking their God for it. Who defines *good* and *evil* in a pluralistic world like ours? And when we disagree about what is evil like we're doing now, who gets to decide? And on what basis do they decide?

Isaac: I don't know the answers to all your questions, but I do know evil when I see it.

Michael: Well, while you're thinking about these questions, here are a few more for you: How do we even know good and evil exist in the first place?

Isaac: Now there's one I don't have to think about. What have you been smoking? Any child knows some things are good and others are bad.

Michael: But maybe their ideas of good and evil are just cultural conventions that change from one society to another. Have you thought of that?

Isaac: No, but I guess I'll have to start.

Michael: I'd recommend it, because if that's what good and evil are, then how can any culture think it has the right to impose its moral ideas on another culture that has its own morality? It all comes down to a question of power.

Isaac: What question of power?

Michael: The question of which culture has the power to impose its morality on others. That's moral imperialism.

Isaac: I have to admit I don't like the sound of that.

Michael: I'm glad to hear it, but there are still more possibilities about what good and evil are. As individual people, maybe good and evil are merely our own personal, private ideas. In that case morality could change not only from one *culture* to another but from one *person* to another. If that's what it is, then how could you say your morality is better than anyone else's? With all these problems, wouldn't we be better off to avoid terms like *good* and *evil* in the first place?

Isaac: Oh yeah, and replace them with what?

Michael: Tolerance and individual rights for all people. Those are the things we should promote, and we should try to avoid anything destructive, like discriminating against other people or imposing our ideas of morality on them. Aren't those the really important things? Just leave it at that. Why complicate matters further with talk of good and evil.

Isaac: I'm confused.

Isaac is not alone. Many people are perplexed by our brave new world, and their questions are the same as Michael's. If we want to stand against evil, what exactly constitutes it and therefore should be eradicated? Who will decide this question when we disagree about it, as we surely will? And what will be their standard of measurement for judging good and evil in a pluralistic culture like ours?

But there are even deeper questions than these. As Michael challenged Isaac, do we know for sure that real good and evil even exist in the first place? Or could it be that concepts like *good* and *evil* are simply defined by one's culture and, consequently, change from one society to another? If so, then there would be no universal standard for judging the morality of actions that could apply across the board. We would have to recognize that whatever moral standard we were using was nothing more than a cultural convention others are free to set aside at will.

Or different still, could it be that morality is purely a personal, private, subjective matter, relative to specific people, situations or times? If that is the case, even cultural definitions of morality are not binding.

How could the president of the United States, or anyone else for that matter, rid the world of a particular case of evil if universal, objective good and evil do not exist in the first place, or if definitions of morality differ from person to person or culture to culture? Who would decide what evil is and when it is gone?

THE MORAL LANDSCAPE HAS RADICALLY CHANGED OVER THE PAST GENERATION.

The president's words implied, of course, that these were not insurmountable problems. His assumption was that there is real good and evil, we can tell the difference, and the attacks on the World Trade Center and Pentagon were clear-cut cases of evil. Surely no one who watched the news that fateful day could doubt his words. Or could they?

Meanwhile, as Michael and Isaac pointed out, in other parts of the world an entirely different sentiment was being expressed. People were rejoicing at the sight of two airliners carrying passengers flying into the twin towers in New York City. This was not only good, they said exuberantly, it was the will of God, and God was to be praised for this attack. Many world citizens were stunned. How could anyone look at something so horrifyingly evil and call it good?

But the reaction of North Americans to this striking act of terrorism was by no means uniform either. Some refused to call this act evil or wrong even as they viewed the gruesome images on their television sets. Like Michael, they preferred words like *inappropriate* or *unacceptable* to describe it. Surely an action like this was out of place. It would be better if it had not happened, but there were just too many problems with labeling the events of 9/11 in these stark moral terms, and some could not bring themselves to do it.

Furthermore, aren't we in the West guilty of our own wrongdoings? Don't we support policies that have caused people in other parts of the world great suffering, even death? If so, how can we now condemn people for fighting back with the only weapons they have? Of course this attack *seemed* wrong to us. We didn't like it. We weren't meant to. But on what basis could we label it evil or wrong? What business did we have imposing our ideas of good and evil onto people thousands of miles away who obviously viewed the world vastly differently than we do?

Meanwhile, the president received widespread support to go to war to search out and destroy those who were behind this act of terrorism.

September 11, 2001, stands out as a day that called forth our deepest gut reactions, our intuitive responses to good and evil, religion, war, terrorism, and to the way humans treat one another. It also brought to light the difficulty we are having engaging others about the moral dilemmas we have created for ourselves. The most basic questions being asked in the days following the attack received different and confusing responses.

Was this attack purely evil or was it actually, in some bizarre sense, good? Of course it was evil, many insisted. What could be worse than hijacking and murdering on a grand scale? Others, however, saw it differently. In their minds this was a necessary response to past aggression.

As Michael also asked, could we even use such stark moral terms as *good* and *evil* to refer to the actions of people from other parts of the world? Yes, we can and should, argued many people. Evil is evil wherever it is found, and if this is not evil then whatever could be? Others disagreed. How could we be so arrogant as to impose our moral perspectives on others? Would we accept *their* moral viewpoints for ourselves? Of course we wouldn't.

And then there was the question of what God must think about this attack. Was God opposed to it, or was he actually in favor of it? The question itself was repugnant to many. If God opposes anything, he must stand against this kind of cruelty, and he will, no doubt, bring the perpetrators to final, ultimate justice. No, responded others to the same question. God was behind this attack, ensuring its success, and he is to be praised for it. The questions continued, and the answers were as astonishing as they were confusing.

This moral maze, while dramatically highlighted by 9/11, extends far beyond the events of that day to a host of other questions and dilemmas. The moral landscape has radically changed in the Western world over the past generation, to the point where it seems almost unrecognizable to those who can view both ends of the past forty years. So-called traditional moral ideas have often been sent packing, replaced by new, sometimes confusing, moral attitudes and a whole set of buzzwords and concepts that go along with them: *tolerance, discrimination, personal autonomy, individual rights, animal rights, human rights, minority rights, gay rights, imposing of values* and *social consensus,* to name a few.

> WE'LL NEVER BE ABLE TO ESCAPE THE MORAL DIMENSIONS OF OUR HUMAN NATURE.

I was struck recently by how new and different our moral landscape has become when I walked by a newsstand one morning and noticed the headlines of a major newspaper: "Wrongful Birth." Since, at the time, this was a new and intriguing term to me, I bought the newspaper and read the story. It told of a woman who was suing the physician who had cared for her during her pregnancy and helped deliver her baby. The child was born with abnormalities that, she claimed, could have been discovered had certain tests been done during the pregnancy. They were not done, and the woman contended that if they had and the abnormalities had been discovered earlier, she would have had an abortion. The child was now four years old, and his mother was suing for wrongful birth.[1]

The article went on to cite other similar cases, and I realized how resolutely our culture is leaving behind a *"sanctity* of life" ethic—in which the value or worth of a human being is based on the simple fact of a per-

---

[1]"Wrongful Birth," *Vancouver Province,* February 19, 1999, p. A4.

son's humanness—and replacing it with a *"quality* of life" ethic, in which a person's value is linked to certain capabilities or qualities he or she has, or to the quality of life he or she could be expected to have. This is a significant cultural change.

It's not that we have thrown out morality altogether. Far from it. We'll never be able to escape the moral dimension of our human nature. Each of us has a moral sense, a conscience, which will continue to exert itself in our thinking and actions. Far from discarding morality altogether, we in the Western world have, if anything, become more morally sensitive in our own selective ways. We continue to forcefully condemn certain activities and attitudes, but we've altered the list of forbidden activities and changed our terminology for condemning them.

Bigotry, intolerance of others' views or chosen lifestyles, condemnation of sexual freedom, discrimination and all violations of human rights are examples of the newly forbidden activities. We condemn them by labeling them *disgusting, inappropriate, despicable, intolerable* or *close-minded,* while studiously avoiding terms like *immoral, good* or *evil.* That was how Michael spoke against the terrorist acts of 9/11 in the preceding conversation. But we shouldn't be fooled by the use of new terms of condemnation. They signify no less denunciation than the old terms. In fact, acts of intolerance, discrimination and the like, while labeled as disgusting and inappropriate, are often treated as the serious moral offenses for which we need to be on the lookout.

On the other hand, tolerance is held up as nearly the supreme moral virtue of our day. Individual rights, especially the right to self-expression, should be promoted for all people, but especially for those who are presently oppressed by governments, corporations and religion, to name a few of the culprits.

But the plot grows more confusing when we realize that these moral directives are not for every situation, because we are also told to have a zero-tolerance policy toward things like drug trafficking, child abuse, bigotry, racism, intolerance and human rights violations of every kind. In fact, it's perfectly OK to impose our moral values on people who do these things and to suspend tolerance toward them. This means that none of these positive values are correct *in principle* but only when applied to the proper situations. Of course, knowing how to recognize these proper situations is precisely what is not always clear.

NEW MORAL MESSAGES

Clearly the moral landscape in Western culture has changed. But what has this change meant for the ordinary person like Isaac who wishes to engage others on moral issues? It has meant that talking about good and bad is no longer simple or clear. New curve balls are being thrown our way, and anyone who has read newspaper editorials, listened to radio talk shows or simply interacted with others has encountered them. The curves thrown are the new and sometimes puzzling moral messages that flow out of the changed moral attitudes dominating Western culture, messages that defy previously accepted ways of thinking about morality. They are being hammered into us from all sides and are adding new twists and turns to the task of engaging others. At times it's hard to even know how to begin because not only is the basis for all moral admonition different but, more importantly, the way we are told to think about our own moral views has dramatically changed.

Notice the way Michael rebuffs Isaac a few days after the previous conversation when Isaac voices his moral disgust about an especially exuberant party held in his residence the night before:

Isaac: I can't believe all the immorality I see in this place!

Michael: Whoa! Hold it right there! Your morality is a personal matter. It's your private morality, and you should keep it that way.

Isaac (taken aback): What does that mean?

Michael: It means your morals are simply expressions of your attitudes and belief system. You have your beliefs, and other people have theirs. What you are calling immoral may be immoral for you but not necessarily for someone else. It's time you finally learn that all people have a right to decide that for themselves.

Isaac (raising his voice): Did you see what was going on here last night at the party?

Michael: Sure I saw it. I was here. Wasn't the turnout great! The night life is finally picking up around here.

Isaac: Yes, there were a lot of people, and if the stuff that happened here wasn't immoral, I'll eat my shirt. I mean did you smell the air in here when it was all over? And did you see those two off in the corner at the end? He looked like he was about to . . .

Michael: Enough already! Sure I saw them, and yes I can smell, and boy have you got some things to learn! What the people at the party were doing only *seemed* immoral to you because you've been taught for so long that it's immoral. I respect your morals and think it's great that you have them. They're probably very good for you, but like I just said, *your* moral values aren't the only ones out there. The world is bigger than the one you come from. We live in a pluralistic, multicultural society, and other people have different ways of looking at the world and of deciding good and evil. You should respect them and their views too.

Isaac (becoming more bullish): Well, where I come from people are straight shooters. We call a spade a spade, and when I see what is obviously immoral I plan on saying so.

Michael: Wrong again. You have no right to impose your moral values on others. Doing that would be intolerant and disrespectful of them and their viewpoints. In fact, it would be downright arrogant. What you're calling "obviously immoral" is nothing more than your personal views on morality. Who are you to say your ideas on morality are right when others plainly have different views of what's right and wrong? You're being exclusionary and close-minded, two things I see the people where you come from don't care much about. Well it's time to start.

Isaac: Apart from your insults, I'm not sure I follow you.

Michael: Apart from my calling a spade a spade, what is not clear?

Isaac: Well, correct me if I'm wrong, but you make it sound like there's no real right or wrong at all. Everybody's ideas are just as good as everybody else's? Is that really what you're saying?

Michael (rolling his eyes): People who think there is *real* right and wrong, as you say, scare me. What they really mean is *their* moral views are right and other people's views are wrong. How arrogant! Who do they think they are?

Isaac: So how does anyone decide what is right and wrong anymore?

Michael: Boy are you a slow learner! There is no real right and wrong, as you like to put it. It's whatever works best for the individual. It's a personal thing. People have to work it out for themselves.

Isaac: Wow! I guess I've got a few things to learn if I'm going to make it here.

Maybe so, but what exactly is Isaac being told to learn? Michael is obviously correct to assert that our society is multicultural and pluralistic, and that other people have different moral values than Isaac's. That's an undeniable demographic fact. Furthermore, showing respect for others who are different from us, as Michael instructs Isaac to do, is certainly good moral instruction. It would be hard to imagine a serious moral code anywhere disagreeing with it.

Why, though, did Michael choose such strong terms to denounce Isaac's attitude toward the people at the party: *intolerant, arrogant, exclusionary* and *close-minded?* Let's make no mistake about it, when people choose potent words like these, it's no accident. In fact, using them is a highly motivational tactic. If Isaac, for instance, can be moved to believe that his own attitudes actually fit these descriptions, he will have great incentive to change. There are certain characteristics most of us just don't want to be told we have and, in fact, could hardly imagine ourselves being guilty of—and these are among them. We would have to be masochistic to *want* to be called intolerant, arrogant or exclusionary.

However, there are some puzzling features of Michael's instruction to

Isaac as well. He has made it clear that Isaac ought not condemn other people's behavior, something Isaac did when commenting on the party at the fraternity house. Michael also declared that it would be wrong for Isaac to impose his moral values on anyone else since other people had different moral views, and Isaac should learn to respect them. Anything less would be arrogance on his part.

What's puzzling is this: Aren't Michael's directives to Isaac moral judgments in themselves? In fact, aren't they outright condemnations of what Isaac was just doing? Michael adamantly asserted that Isaac's condemning attitude of the people at the party was wrong and that he ought to change it. In fact, Isaac's entire understanding of morality should be changed, according to Michael, because it led him to be arrogant, intolerant and close-minded, and these are characteristics he should not have.

Furthermore, hasn't Michael just imposed his own moral code on Isaac, even while telling him he should not impose his morality on others? Michael has listed a number of activities Isaac ought to stop doing. It turns out that declarations like "you ought not condemn other people's actions" and "you should not impose your moral values on others" are self-defeating. In the very act of making these statements, the person commits the precise error he or she is telling others not to commit.

It seems equally puzzling that Michael told Isaac his morality is personal and private and should stay that way, and in the next breath told him he ought to act in a way that is respectful and tolerant of others. Is the directive that Isaac should be respectful and tolerant toward other people Michael's own moral view? If so, he should have kept it to himself since, according to his admonition to Isaac, his own morality too must be a personal and private matter. What business did he have then dictating his moral views to Isaac?

In other words, given his own moral views, Michael was not in a position to tell Isaac he should show respect or tolerance or anything else toward others. But as we saw, he had plenty of moral instructions for Isaac, all of which violated his own moral code.

When we stop to think about it, short of ceasing to comment on moral matters altogether (something Michael has not done in this dialogue), how are we to carry out Michael's understanding of morality? It appears Isaac is being told to act in a way that is at the very least incoherent and at worst impossible. Michael may need to make some modifications to his moral views as he continues to formulate them, at least if he hopes he or others will be able to live by them. But whatever the difficulties may be with the moral perspectives advocated by Michael in this dialogue, they have not prevented them from being widely accepted in our culture. Indeed, this way of thinking about moral matters has become popular and fashionable, and it has had a far-reaching influence on our culture.

> **DECLARATIONS LIKE "YOU OUGHT NOT CONDEMN OTHER PEOPLE'S ACTIONS" AND "YOU SHOULD NOT IMPOSE YOUR MORAL VALUES ON OTHERS" ARE SELF-DEFEATING.**

Moral philosopher Christina Hoff Sommers, commenting on this influence, has written that the wide acceptance of this moral perspective has not only left us with few firm moral principles to guide us through the tough moral questions we face, but it has also produced a generation of people who not only have trouble distinguishing right from wrong but who actually question whether such standards exist at all.[2]

Sommers contends that we have been thrown back to a moral stone age, and she points to the present generation of university students as evidence. She observes that when students come to a university, there are many wonderful things about most of them. They are good-hearted, fairminded, generous and decent. They form wonderful friendships and an astonishing number of them do volunteer work, far more than their baby-boomer parents ever did. They donate blood in record numbers,

---

[2]Christina Hoff Sommers, *Imprimus* 27, no. 3 (1998): 1-3.

they help with Meals On Wheels, and they give up summer vacations to work with deaf children. As a university professor myself, I fully concur and have seen these types of volunteer activities carried out by my students many times.

However, Sommers continues, ask one of these young people if there are such things as real right and wrong, and suddenly you will be confronted with a confused, tongue-tied individual. The same person who works with Meals On Wheels and volunteers for a suicide-prevention hotline might give you an answer like the one Michael gave to Isaac when he asked him how anyone could decide what was right and wrong: "Well, there really is no such thing as real right and wrong. It's kind of like whatever works best for the individual. Each person has to work it out for himself." That answer is common in our culture. This should disturb us because it is no better than the moral philosophy, if we dare call it that, of a psychopath, a person for whom moral concepts and considerations play no part in decision-making processes.

Whatever we think of this confusing sea change, the challenge for us is to come to grips with it, to understand the changing moral climate we all live and breathe. Unless we do, we will never genuinely hear and engage others. Rather, our attempts to talk about good and evil will be nothing more than occasions for talking past each other.

But changes to the moral landscape have come from an entirely new and unexpected source as well, and that is the exploding technology in the Western world. Who would have thought that wonderful technological advancements that continually amaze and delight us would also bring with them new and challenging moral dilemmas. How is this possible, and what does it mean for anyone desiring to talk about good and evil? It means engaging others has become a more complex task than we perhaps realized. It's time for us to explore these new complexities.

3

TECHNO-PERIL

New Technologies, New Moral Dilemmas

Perhaps you have heard the story of the pilot who announced over the plane's PA system: "This is your captain speaking. We are presently flying at thirty thousand feet above sea level and traveling at six hundred miles per hour. I have some good news and some bad news. The good news is we're making excellent time. The bad news is we're lost."

If I were a passenger on that pilot's plane, I would not be comforted by any part of his announcement. Even the part that was supposed to be "good news" is hardly good under these circumstances. Making excellent time is usually a desirable thing, but what is the use of doing so if we're lost? In fact, do we even *want* to be making excellent time if we're lost? Wouldn't it be preferable to come to a stop and figure out the right way to go before proceeding any further? For all we know, we could be heading precisely in the wrong direction and moving further from where we want to go. Of course, stopping to ask for directions is not an easy thing to do when flying an airliner. Neither is it in some other areas of life.

However much we may chuckle at this pilot's announcement, it does express the serious dilemma facing us in this new millennium. Technologically, we're making excellent time. In fact, we are moving forward at breathtaking speed. New devices, instruments, gadgets, conveniences and techniques for going about life's business appear virtually on a daily basis. They surround us and affect most every part of our lives. We warm up leftovers in the kitchen differently because of microwave technology. We communicate with colleagues and friends around the globe at lightning speed using electronic communications. GPS systems in our cars can give us step-by-step directions to our destinations without ever having to stop to ask for directions. Even if we don't have GPS, stopping is not necessary; we simply make a call on our cell phone and carry on. Medical procedures that used to require days in the hospital are now often

NEW TECHNOLOGICAL CAPABILITIES BRING WITH THEM EQUALLY NEW ETHICAL QUESTIONS.

performed in a matter of hours with the patient returning home the same day, thanks to our continually improving medical technology.

Morally, however, it sometimes seems as though we're lost. The developments in modern technology have been outstripping our ability to understand their ethical implications, especially the long-range ones. As we go about our business using our new laptops, PDAs, camera phones, MRI machines and high-tech guidance systems, we easily forget that new technologies do not arise in a vacuum. There are ethical implications of developing and using them, many of which are both serious and unavoidable. This is because new technological capabilities bring with them equally new ethical questions that, like the technologies themselves, were unimaginable just a few years ago.

The result for us in the West has been that not only is the number of ethical dilemmas confronting us on the increase, but the complexity of these dilemmas is as well. This is the new world, and ethically it is very different from the old one, thanks to our technology. Talking about good and evil with those around us has just taken on a new and complicated twist.

Imagine the following conversation between Michael, who is very enthused about recent technological advances, and Isaac, who is not so sure:

Michael: Isn't technology great! We're living in amazing times. What a world!

Isaac: Yes, it is quite a world. But excuse me if I don't share your unmitigated enthusiasm for technology.

Michael: Don't tell me you're a technophobe?

Isaac: A what?

Michael: A technophobe, a person who has an irrational fear of technology, which leads him or her to hate it.

Isaac: I don't hate technology. I use it all the time and appreciate a lot of it. But I'm willing to admit it's a two-edged sword, something I see you're not willing to concede. It sometimes ends up causing harm along with the good—and sometimes serious harm.

Michael: Listen, Mr. Pessimist, do you know what technology has allowed us to do? Medical technology alone has brought marvelous benefits to our health and well-being. CAT scans. MRIs. Laser surgery. Respirators. Oxygen machines. It goes on and on. People no longer need to die from polio or pneumonia, thanks to these new technologies. Our great-grandparents couldn't even imagine these medical treatments.

Isaac: Maybe they were the lucky ones.

Michael: Did I hear you right? What do you mean *they* were the lucky ones? In their day people died from polio and pneumonia. How is that lucky? Not long before that, even common infections could kill. Today our medical therapies have taken the sting out of many diseases and disorders, and technology has provided these therapies. Please tell me you know that!

Isaac: Yes, I do, which is why I wonder if they were the lucky ones. Are you aware of the other side of these treatments?

Michael: What other side?

Isaac: That sometimes they come at a high cost to suffering people. Put yourself in the shoes of a cancer sufferer who is near death's door and who suddenly gets pneumonia. In his condition it could end his life. Ask yourself if you would want your death postponed? By surviving the pneumonia with the help of modern medical technology, you would be left to suffer in increasingly agonizing conditions because now your cancer has been given more time to work its full ravages on you while you await your inevitable death anyway. Is that really so wonderful?

Michael: Only you could manage to make something as wonderful as a cure for pneumonia sound bad.

Isaac: Actually, I'm not alone. Plenty of people don't think it's wonderful at all. In fact, the prospect of suffering this way, at one's most vulnerable point in life, has caused many people, particularly elderly people, to become terrified of what old age may hold for them and of what the medical profession, armed with its mighty technology, could do to them once they're at it's mercy.

Michael: Why not just give them or their families a choice? Let them use the medical technology if they want to but refuse it if they don't?

Isaac: They have that choice now. No one is forced to accept medical treatment.

Michael: Then I don't see a problem.

Isaac: You might if you put yourself in the shoes of the family of the suffering person or even the attending physician who now has to make that choice: either use the medical equipment to help the patient survive the pneumonia or refuse to use it and watch her die. Think about it. What are the chances that you would say no to the medical technology that could bring *your* loved one through her illness when it's right there available to you?

Michael: OK, I see your point.

Isaac: The fact that it's available and ready to use has put the choice of whether to use it in our hands, and it's hard to refuse. It seems unthinkable to watch a loved one die when you have the ability to prevent it. But like I said, it often becomes a two-edged sword because the patient pulls through, which at first sounds wonderful, but only to go on to new levels of suffering and anguish that they never would have endured if the technology had not enabled them to survive. That's why we used to call pneumonia . . .

Michael: Yes, I know, the old man's friend.

Isaac: That's right. It used to end elderly people's lives before other more serious diseases were given the time to eat away at them and destroy their quality of life further. But now we don't allow it to be the "friend" it once was, thanks to our technology.

Michael: So new medical technology is a double-edged sword. I'll have to process that idea for a while.

Isaac: While you're processing, you should know that it's a two-edged sword for another reason as well.

Michael: What other reason?

Isaac: It has also produced a whole new set of difficult moral dilemmas.

Michael: How does technology do that?

Isaac: By giving us more capabilities.

Michael: Well, that is the whole point of new technology, to enable us to do things we couldn't do before.

Isaac: I agree. So far, so good. But what we may not have noticed is that any time we *can* do something, we are suddenly forced to ask whether we *ought* to do it. It's the moral question, and technology has given us a whole set of these that we didn't have before, some of which are exceedingly complicated and controversial.

Michael: Such as?

Isaac: Think about the people we were just talking about, patients near the end of life who we can now keep alive far longer than we ever could before—and often with terrible conditions that most of us would never want to live with. This confronts us with an ethical question.

Michael: Which is . . . ?

Isaac: Now that we *can* keep these people alive far longer, *should* we do it just because we can? Here's how our ethics professor put it to us just last week: Is there actually a moral *obligation,* not just a *choice,* to keep people alive for as long as we possibly can in any and every condition?

Michael: I hardly think so. Doing that would only prolong the dying process and increase suffering in the process. Surely the purpose of our medical technology is not to do that.

Isaac: Good point. That was the professor's answer too, and many people agree with it. But there are plenty of people who think we fallible human beings have no business deciding when other human beings should live or die.

Michael: I guess they have a right to their opinion.

Isaac: How magnanimous of you, Michael. But that's only the beginning of the questions for people like this. What if the person has actually asked us to disconnect him from life support so that he can die? Should we honor his wish if we are convinced that doing so will bring about his death? Is this not the same as killing him at his request? But that leads to another question. What if we decide to go ahead and honor his request and disconnect him, but then, lo and behold, he continues to live anyway? Should we then offer him a lethal injection with the assistance of a physician to help him die gently and peacefully as he desires?

Michael: You mean offer him a physician-assisted suicide?

Isaac: Yes, our medical technology has forced us to confront this question, and as you know, there is great controversy over it in our society. And we're still hardly touching the tip of the iceberg.

Michael: What iceberg?

Isaac: The iceberg of ethical questions brought on by exploding technology. Thanks to new technology, we are now facing moral questions concerning stem-cell research, cloning, fetal-tissue research, weapons of mass destruction . . .

Michael: Whoa! You mean atomic bombs, hydrogen bombs, chemical weapons and biological weapons?

Isaac: Exactly. These are purely the result of technological advancement. If we didn't know how to build them, we would never need to ask whether we should use them, and if so, when and under what conditions. Now we have no choice but to confront these questions too. Our brave new world of technology is filled with ethical dilemmas.

Michael: I'm not sure I want to talk about this anymore.

Michael is not alone in his reluctance to raise issues like these. Sometimes talking about them is not only a complicated process but a contentious one as well. The point of his discussion with Isaac is that for all its wonders and benefits, technology also confronts us with new and perplexing dilemmas that we never had to think about before it existed. And there are far more dilemmas than the ones raised by Isaac and Michael. When there was nothing we could do to save the lives of unborn babies whose brains had died inside the bodies of their mothers, we didn't have to decide what our moral duty was to these unborn babies or their mothers. Before organ transplantation existed, we didn't have to ask which person deserved an available organ when more than one person needed it. Now we have no choice but to face these questions and a multitude of others like them.

Technology has always had this unintended consequence. There was a time when no muskets or rifles existed, not to mention atomic, hydrogen, chemical and biological weapons. In that time we didn't have to think about whether it was ever morally acceptable to use these "new" means of fighting our wars. There was also a time when there were no automobiles. No one had to ask how a car ought to be used and what should or shouldn't be done with it. Lest we think these are unimportant questions, it is worth noting that probably no invention has affected our lifestyle and maybe even our values more than the automobile. To see this, all we have to do is imagine life without automobiles and paved highways, auto-manufacturing plants, gas stations, used-car sales people, service shops, jobs and government revenues that exist as a direct result of the automobile.

Today, our new and vast technological capabilities confront us with burdensome ethical dilemmas, and this fact raises a fundamental question: *Should* every conceivable technological capability be developed merely because we have the means to develop it? Does the simple fact that we *can* do something automatically give us the moral permission to do it? Or should we hold the line on certain proposed technologies and refuse to develop them as simply not worth the risks and thorny choices they will create? In other words, might we actually be better off without certain technological abilities in our hands, even ones we are perfectly capable of developing?

That is a hard question because the reality is that technology tends to act like a virtual steamroller. It rolls unstoppably forward, crushing every obstacle and "old" way of doing things in its path. Ease and efficiency become the new gods, and no objection is able to stand in the way of progress. When questions are raised about the value or legitimacy of a particular new technological capability, the questioners are often berated as dinosaurs and told to get their heads out of the sand and join the rest of us in the new millennium.

One prominent ethicist has issued his own warning that technology creates its own imperative. "If we can do it, we will do it," he has written.[1] He has a point. Consider Michael's enthusiasm over what our technology now enables us to do in the realm of end-of-life care that only a few decades ago we could not have done. And think of the pressure to use this technology to help suffering people. Who would stand in the way of developing or using technology to prolong life? Aren't such capabilities wonderful?

But as Isaac pointed out, the other side of this new technology is its unintended side effect of causing greater suffering. All too often, surviving pneumonia has meant giving cancer, multiple sclerosis, ALS or some other terminal or progressive condition more time to work its full ravages on an ill person's body. Rather than stopping death with new medical advances, we are merely putting it on hold, often leaving people to suffer in increasingly agonizing and fearful circumstances while they await the inevitable. With each passing day or week, they become weaker and groggier as their pain-management needs increase, which makes them less able to communicate with loved ones. For people like this, the new technology sometimes feels like a mixed blessing at best.

As Isaac pointed out, this has caused many people, particularly the elderly or ill, to become terrified of what the medical profession might do to them with its technology. Medical science, armed with high-powered technology, is no longer automatically seen as a friend. Some of the very people who need and depend on it the most have come to fear it.

How has it come to this? Through a surprising chain of events dating back well over a century. During the first half and into the second half of the last century, medical science conquered many illnesses, such as small pox and polio, and controlled many more, such as diabetes. As one physician has written, "the public, steeped in Hollywood's Dr. Kildare and Marcus Welby, subconsciously began to feel that the science of medicine would eventually conquer death itself. In pursuit of this elusive dream, the medical profession, hand in hand with an adoring, credulous public, developed the credo that anything and everything to prolong and extend

---

[1]Peter Singer, *Rethinking Life and Death* (New York: St. Martin's Press, 1994), p. 19.

life must always be done."[2] What could be better than this?

Then technology caught up with us, and we began to realize its effects on our most vulnerable citizens. No wonder many are fearful of what old age may hold for them in the hands of a medical profession equipped with new and powerful technologies. The result has been that many have written living wills as a way to try to control the uncontrollable. Others have gone further and requested physician-assisted suicide. As much as we all want to live, at least this way we can feel like we are retaining some control over the way and time we die.

> **ANY TIME WE CAN DO SOMETHING, WE ARE SUDDENLY FORCED TO ASK WHETHER WE OUGHT TO DO IT.**

But these responses have created their own ethical dilemmas. Does there ever come a time when we should let someone die? It seems, to most of us at least, that there is such a time. The simple recognition that (1) we all will die sooner or later, (2) we cannot postpone death forever, and (3) trying to do so in every case will merely increase suffering for some people and may involve force-feeding medication to people who do not wish to receive it, has led us to give patients the legal right to refuse medical treatments if they wish. That is the law.

What then do we do with the person Isaac spoke of who requests to be disconnected from her life support systems because she sees no point in continuing the fight, but who then continues to live once disconnected? And what if she made the request believing full well that she

---

[2]Arnold Voth, "Euthanasia—A Physician's Definitions and Critiques," unpublished paper presented at Regent College, Vancouver, June 26, 1993. Voth further develops the notion that new medical technologies have driven many people to fear what the medical profession may do to them at their most vulnerable moments and to see physician-assisted suicide as the only way to regain control of their destinies.

would die? In fact, she wanted to die because, for her, life had become worse than death. Everything that once gave her enjoyment in life has now been taken away. And what if she now went the next step and actually asked us to assist her in ending her own life?

This opens the debate over physician-assisted suicide. Should we legalize this practice and grant this person's wish in the name of respect for personal autonomy, or should we refuse to legalize or to give assistance in the name of protecting other elderly, disabled or ill people from being put in a position where their own continued existence now becomes a choice they must make? At present, most Western nations are deeply divided about which of these responses is the correct one to make.

Meanwhile issues such as fetal-tissue research have forced us to confront questions like how *person* should be defined. Must a person actually *function* as a person with consciousness, self-awareness, communication and reasoning ability and the like in order to *be* a person? If so, then obviously a fetus could never qualify, and we would have no moral obligation to treat it like a person. However, if *function* is the determining criterion for personhood, it's hard to see how a newborn baby qualifies as a person, or a normal thirty-five-year-old adult who happens to be sleeping or is in a reversible coma for that matter.

But if these *are* indeed persons, even though they are not *functioning* as persons, then obviously there is a more fundamental determining criterion for personhood than function. We are implicitly appealing to the existence of latent capacities that exist but are nonfunctional at the moment as the determining criterion. Because the capabilities are there, this being is a person.

But if this is the correct criterion for personhood, then it is difficult to see why an unborn human being does not qualify as a tiny, developing person with all the capacities for personhood present even though he or she is in embryonic, nonfunctional form at the moment. These capacities don't need to be inserted later, only allowed to develop further into functional form.

Whatever else we think of our exploding technology, we must come to grips with the fact that it has made the task of talking about good and bad far more complex than before. Furthermore, the combination of breathtaking technological advances and new moral messages has had a deep and disorienting effect on our culture that no one could have predicted. It constitutes a double whammy for those wishing to engage the moral issues of our day. How do we resolve or engage others on these tough moral dilemmas in the midst of new and often puzzling moral thinking?

Our culture is in transition. It is in the process of rejecting one approach to morality and searching for a replacement along the lines advocated by Michael in the preceding dialogue. And it's been a rough ride. We have ended up with profound moral confusion at the deepest levels of our moral thinking. As we collectively wrestle with our moral dilemmas, this confusion has affected not only individuals but our culture as a whole. Few things can make moral discussion more mystifying than encountering statements and perspectives that just don't seem to make sense to us. If we want to engage others effectively on important moral issues, we must understand and untangle the web of confusion surrounding them.

4

OUTPOSTS IN OUR HEADS

Understanding the Moral Confusion

Our society is morally confused!" The person who uttered those words to me was not merely asserting that he saw immorality around him. Of course he saw that. It has always been there, and in that sense it is hardly worth mentioning. What this person was claiming to see in Western society was something different, something he called moral confusion.

However we may initially react to a statement like this, it's worth noting that even the well-known philosopher Peter Singer, himself an advocate of moving away from traditional moral thinking, recognizes that if we do, the journey is, in his words, "bound to be filled with uncertainty and confusion."[1] Singer appears to be correct in his prediction, and thanks to the confusion he speaks of, engaging others in discussion of moral issues in our culture has become increasingly unpredictable, even disorienting. If you have chosen to get involved in such discussions at all, you've probably had the experience of watching one of your conversations go sideways for reasons you could not quite understand, and you were left shaking your head, wondering what

---

[1]Peter Singer, *Rethinking Life and Death* (New York: St. Martin's Press, 1994), p. 4.

went wrong. Things were said which just didn't seem to fit.

If we are to engage others successfully on the moral issues confronting our culture, it is imperative that we recognize moral confusion when we encounter it and then be able to sort through it. But what does moral confusion look like, and how does it show up in our society? As we will see, it comes in more than one variety.

SAME PERSON: CONFLICTING MORAL VIEWS

One form of moral confusion occurs when clashing moral views are held within a person's mind. This condition of *same person: conflicting moral views,* is not the same as simple moral disagreement between people. Anyone who thinks carefully about the social issues of our day will come to hold viewpoints on a variety of moral questions such as war, the environment, stem-cell research, human cloning, abortion, physician-assisted suicide, animal rights and a host of others. These issues are controversial, and whatever our views on them, they will differ from the views of some other people we interact with. This kind of moral disagreement on contentious social issues comes with the territory, and we should expect it. Interpersonal moral disagreement doesn't necessarily indicate moral confusion as much as it reflects the reality that moral dilemmas are often hard to resolve, and people approach them from fundamentally different perspectives.

But what if the conflicting viewpoints, rather than existing in the minds of two or more different people, are both found in the mind of one and the same person? When that happens, we no longer have a case of moral disagreement between people. This kind of cognitive moral dissonance reflects serious moral confusion.

But how could this happen? How could one person hold two opposing viewpoints or assumptions at the same time? Envision the following interchange between Michael and Isaac on an issue that has brought this kind of moral confusion to light more than most others.

Isaac: Can you believe this news story? I had no idea this was going on in our own country.

Michael: You had no idea *what* was going on? This is a great country. How bad can your news story be?

Isaac (shaking his head): It's bad. All across the country, people prefer baby boys over girls . . .

Michael: Boy, are you uptight! What's wrong with hoping for a boy—or a girl, for that matter?

Isaac: Nothing is wrong with *hoping*, but that's not where it stops. According to this story some pregnant women across this country who hope their babies are male rather than female are having amniocenteses done at their local hospitals.

Michael: So what's the problem? Amniocentesis is a very effective procedure to determine the health of the baby before it's born. It's wonderful that women can get these.

Isaac: But that's not why these women are getting them.

Michael: Why then?

Isaac: They're having this procedure performed to find out the sex of the child.

Michael: You mean *that's* what you're uptight about!? You'd better join us in the twenty-first century. That is common practice now.

Isaac: No, that's not what I'm "uptight" about. These women are asking for abortions. That's why they're having the amniocenteses, and that's what I'm uptight about, as you like to put it. How atrocious can people get! I've always been against abortion but this . . . this is outrageous! How far will the pro-choice movement go? Will these people stop at nothing?

Michael: Now wait just a minute. Don't pin this on all pro-choice people. I'm pro-choice, and I don't agree with this practice at all, nor would most pro-choice people I know. Aborting because the fetus is female is just plain wrong!

Isaac: I'm confused. How can you call it wrong? You just said you're pro-choice. Don't you believe women have a right to choose? Isn't that your mantra?

Michael: Of course women have a right to choose, but aborting because the fetus is female is sexist. It's antiwomen, and most of us in the pro-choice movement would have no part of it.

Isaac: I'm beginning to think one of us is confused, but I'm not sure it's me anymore.

Isaac is not the only one who has been taken aback by this true story. When it broke, an immediate hue and cry arose from many quarters, including numerous newspaper editorialists, philosophers and ethicists. The response of pro-life groups and individuals was not surprising. Like Isaac, they condemned this practice in no uncertain terms. It is outrageous. The real problem for them, however, isn't that female fetuses are targeted. In fact, as revolting as this reason for aborting an unborn child is to pro-life people, morally speaking, it's irrelevant. The real problem is simply that these are abortions, and abortion is murder.

But what really caught my eye was the response of people and groups who are known to support abortion rights. Like Michael in the dialogue, many of these people condemn this practice as well. Targeting female fetuses for abortions is wrong, they said, and should be stopped.

But how could they condemn it, I wondered? Why would they? After all, they are pro-choice, and if being pro-choice means anything, it means standing for the right of women to choose abortions for their own reasons, free of the restrictions and constraints of others. And that's just what the pregnant women in this story were doing, choosing to have abortions for their own reasons. The fact that you or I may not like those reasons is precisely what does not matter from the pro-choice perspective. If we don't think their reasons are legitimate, then *we* need not have abortions for those reasons. That is our choice, but we have no right to impose our choices on anyone else. That's the point of being pro-choice. How then could people with this view denounce this practice?[2]

Their reason for condemning it is astonishing and confusing. Like Michael, they said that having abortions for this reason is wrong because it's sexist. Targeting female fetuses and aborting them specifically because they are female is antiwomen, and it must end.[3]

But we must ask, how can this practice be antiwomen if the fetus is not a person to begin with? After all, the most fundamental argument for abortion, or perhaps I should say the most foundational assumption behind all arguments for abortion, is that the fetus is not a person and according to some pro-choice advocates not human at all until well into the pregnancy. Dr. Henry Morgentaler, prominent Canadian abortion-rights activist and Auschwitz survivor, speaks for this viewpoint in his description of human life at its earliest stage. "At conception," writes Morgentaler, "two half-cells, an ovum and a sperm, unite to create one whole cell. Surely common sense alone tells us that this single cell isn't a human being, at least not in any sense that we normally use the term."[4]

Philosopher Mary Anne Warren, a well-known abortion-rights advocate, agrees and argues forcefully that the fetus, while obviously a human in the *biological* sense, is not one in the *moral* sense. In other words, it doesn't have the moral rights or obligations that humans in this moral sense (that is, as persons) have since it doesn't have the capacities that Warren believes define personhood (membership in the moral community). These consist of reasoning ability, self-awareness, communicative powers, self-motivated activity and so forth. Her conclusion is that fetuses simply are not persons, and we have no moral obligation to treat

---

[2]This is the view commonly expressed by members of the pro-choice community.

[3]The problem of gender-targeted abortions has driven the Indian minister for medical health and family welfare, Raja Mahendra Aridaman Singh, to direct officers in his government to strictly enforce the Female Foeticide Act. The Act has specific provision of imprisonment and fines for those who, after a sex-determination test, kill the female fetus. See India's *Times News Network*, May 31, 2002.

[4]Henry Morgentaler, *Abortion & Contraception* (New York: Beaufort Books, 1982), p. 143.

them as though they were. This of course means that the right to life that human persons have doesn't apply to the fetus. The mother's rights and wishes always take precedence.[5]

The problem, however, is that if a fetus is not a human or a person, then a *female* fetus is not one either. We simply can't say that it is morally permissible to abort fetuses because they are not humans or persons, but that it is *not* permissible to abort them *if you do so because they are female* since that would be antiwomen. If they are not humans or persons at all, how does our treatment of them translate into poor treatment of women? Indeed, this is the whole point of the argument supporting abortion: because fetuses are not persons, women should be free to choose an abortion for any reason whatsoever. No person is being hurt in an abortion because the fetus is neither a human nor a person. Human rights simply do not apply to fetuses, at least in their early stages of development.

It looks as if there is a clash of moral views going on in the minds of pro-choice people who wish to condemn this practice as antiwomen while at the same time upholding the right to abortion on demand. They will have to choose which moral viewpoint to hold. On one hand, something tells us it is wrong to target female fetuses for abortions. On the other hand, our arguments for abortion undercut any objection we could have to this practice. Either abortions, including this kind, are justified because the fetus is not a person, or gender-driven abortions are antiwomen and, hence, wrong. If they are indeed antiwomen, then the fetus has far greater moral status than that accorded to it by the pro-choice movement when it advocates abortion on demand. And many more abortions than just these few gender-driven ones must be called into question. Holding both viewpoints is a case of moral confusion. The reaction to gender-driven abortions has brought this confusion to light.

---

[5]Mary Anne Warren, "On the Moral and Legal Status of Abortion," *The Monist* 57, no. 1 (1973). In this article Warren chides her pro-choice colleagues for using other arguments to support abortion rights while putting little effort into arguing for this basic premise, that the fetus is not a person. She asserts that all arguments are unpersuasive as long as this fundamental pro-life assumption is left unchallenged. She then proceeds to argue against this assumption in an attempt to make a viable case for the moral permissibility of abortion.

SAME SOCIETY: CONFLICTING MORAL VIEWS

Sometimes, however, the conflicting views are not limited to the minds of *individual people*. Occasionally *society* at large holds irreconcilable views and attempts to act on them. The results are not only confusing but often tragic. This is illustrated in the case of two New Jersey teenage sweethearts, Amy Grossberg and Brian Peterson, who left a school dance to check into a motel room. There they delivered their baby boy and threw him into the trash can where he was left to die. Later the two went to court for this action, were found guilty of manslaughter and received jail terms. In addition, they faced the condemnation of the national media and the nation at large, and received a harsh lecture from the judge. "There's a disturbing aspect to your character," he sternly declared, "an egocentrism . . . that blinded you to the intrinsic value of the life of your child."[6]

But one columnist expressed the bewilderment felt by many at the societal reaction. "The puzzling thing is this," he wrote. "Had the couple decided to end Grossberg's inconvenient pregnancy by abortion, the same society that passed such stern moral judgment on them would have gone out of its way to facilitate their choice. . . . We claim to condemn Grossberg and her boyfriend for their callous selfishness, for ridding themselves of an inconvenience at the cost of another's life," he continued, "when in fact we're only condemning them for not employing the socially approved method for doing so." This commentator called the reaction by the judge and society "moral insanity."[7] It was a case of society trying to act on two conflicting moral viewpoints, the intrinsic value of human life and the desire to have abortion on demand, and the result was both sad and confusing.

The same conflicting assumptions across society are evident in the widespread use of diagnostic testing on pregnant women and their unborn children. This is especially obvious when the testing is combined with expectations of treatment for developing children in utero. Is the baby that is being diagnosed a patient with rights and interests that

---

[6]This story was written by George Jonas and syndicated by Southam News in Canada in July 1998.

[7]These comments are included in the same editorial by George Jonas.

should be protected, or is it something far less, a fetus without such rights, which can be aborted at will?

Prenatal diagnostic treatments often make conflicting assumptions about this question. For example, the prospect of treating certain conditions in the womb suggests the unborn child is regarded as a person with interests that we can and ought to protect. On the other hand, it is widely assumed that if a test shows up signs of genetic abnormality, such as Down syndrome or spina bifida, the pregnancy will be terminated. This at least implicitly regards the genetically defective unborn child as less than a full person. Which is it?[8]

The fact is, we all tend to believe and simply assume that our views on one moral question do not inadvertently clash with our views on another. Clearly for many of us this is not the case, but it usually takes a particular event, such as the case of gender-driven abortions or the New Jersey sweethearts, to bring this internal clash to light. When this happens, hard decisions must be made. If two moral principles really do conflict with each other, one will cancel out the other.

> **THE PROSPECT OF TREATING CERTAIN CONDITIONS IN THE WOMB SUGGESTS THE UNBORN CHILD IS REGARDED AS A PERSON WITH INTERESTS THAT WE CAN AND OUGHT TO PROTECT.**

Even if we try to hold two conflicting views at the same time and claim that such contradictions do not really matter, the realities of life won't allow us to live this way. When push comes to shove in the hard cases, we'll have to decide which viewpoints we really believe and which we are will-

---

[8]J. P. Moreland and Scott Rae, *Body & Soul: Human Nature and the Crisis in Ethics* (Downers Grove, Ill.: InterVarsity Press, 2000), p. 290. See also pp. 299-300 where Moreland and Rae give further evidence of conflicting moral assumptions at work in bioethical decisions and practices in North America.

ing to abandon. Our actions will tell the story of what we have decided.

WHEN OUR APPROACH TO MORALITY BECOMES CONFUSED

The moral confusion, however, is deeper than merely *clashing views on particular moral questions*. If we leave aside specific cases and consider the very *approach* our culture has begun to take to moral questions, we will see that our whole way of doing morality has become confused and contradictory.

On one hand, our culture is fully prepared to forcefully condemn certain forbidden activities: child abuse, rape, intolerance, bigotry, discrimination, the imposition of one's moral views on others and suppression of human rights, to name a few of the most common suspects. On the other hand, huge numbers of us have embraced a moral philosophy that has come to be called *moral relativism*. This is not a new phenomenon and many have written about it, but I wonder if we realize how greatly this dual approach contributes to our culture's moral confusion.

Notice the way Michael enthusiastically explains his own newfound moral relativism to Isaac who meets him coming out of his ethics class:

Isaac: Hey Michael. Where are you coming from with all those books?

Michael: Our ethics class just ended, and these are our textbooks: Aristotle, Frankena, Holmes, Sterba, Singer, Warren. This professor has us reading ideas I've never heard of.

Isaac: Whoa! Whoa! What ideas? I have to admit that before this semester began and I got into my own ethics class, I was really curious about what goes on in a class like that and why anyone would take one. I took it because it was required for my program. But it always seemed to me that what's right is right and what's wrong is wrong. We learn most of it way before we ever get to university.

Michael: Boy, you do need a course in ethics don't you! For one thing, you might learn to be more careful about what and who you call *right* and *wrong*. You're still playing fast and loose with those words, and if you'll remember what I said before . . .

Isaac: OK, OK, if this is your "you should respect other people's morals because yours aren't the only ones" lecture, don't bother because I've heard it before.

Michael: I know you've heard it, but it's pretty obvious you didn't get it.

Isaac: What I don't get is why you make such a big fuss over the fact that my morals aren't the only ones. I know they're not. I just happen to disagree with some of the moral ideas out there. Is that a crime?

Michael: And I presume that when you disagree with someone else's morality, you're right and the other person is wrong?

Isaac: I guess I could be wrong sometimes too.

Michael: That's very magnanimous of you, Isaac.

Isaac: Humility has always been my greatest virtue.

Michael: Indeed, but as a matter of fact, you may have been too fast in admitting you could be wrong in your moral viewpoints.

Isaac: Would you make up your mind!

Michael: I have. The reason I keep saying we need to respect others' moral views when we disagree with them is that neither of us is really wrong. That's the part of the "lecture" you may not have heard before.

Isaac (dripping with sarcasm): Are you serious? Two people disagree and both are right? Nobody's wrong? How sweet it is! What can that possibly mean?

Michael: It means that the truth of moral judgments depends on the attitude or opinion of the person making them. That's why two people can both be right even when they disagree. It's also why you need to be more careful about calling people wrong just because they disagree with you.

Isaac: Is this what you're learning from Aristotle? Funny, I had him figured differently.

Michael: Well, no. Aristotle is really quite old-fashioned in these matters, as seen in his *Nicomachean Ethics*. We're reading him just to pick his theories apart and compare them to some more up-to-date ideas on morality.

Isaac: Well, I believe moral statements are either true or false. I guess that's where you and I part company.

Michael: As a matter of fact, I agree with you.

Isaac: How can you? You just said . . .

Michael: I know what I said. I can because the truth of moral statements is determined by the person making them. Like I said, it depends on his attitude, opinion or belief system. His moral statements may be true for him even though they are not for you, if your attitude or beliefs are different.

Isaac: Are you seriously telling me that a moral statement could be true for someone else but not for me?

Michael: Yes.

Isaac: I suppose you're also going to tell me that you and I could make moral statements that are opposites and both could be true?

Michael: Of course. One is true for you, and the other is true for me.

Isaac: You keep saying that.

Michael: It's beautiful! No more condemning other people or imposing our moral values on them, or even thinking they are wrong just because they have different moral views than ours. Hey brother, it's the way to peace and harmony. I knew this ethics class would be good, but I didn't know it would be *this* good.

Michael is not alone in his enthusiasm for moral relativism. Indeed, it has become fashionable moral thinking in Western culture. But what exactly is it? Moral relativism comes in a number of forms, but essentially it is the position that asserts there are no objectively true moral values that apply to all people and situations consistently. The operative word here, of course, is *objective,* and it's important to understand precisely what this word means. What are we asserting about something when we label it "objective"?

To answer this question, consider its opposite term, *subjective.* Examples of *subjectively* true statements are: "This mocha is good," or "That squid is bad." We often utter statements like these, but what precisely are we saying when we do? At first glance, we seem to be saying something about mochas or squid, but on closer inspection it becomes clear that we really aren't. Rather, these statements really mean "I like this mocha," or "I don't like that squid," and as such, the statements are saying something about the person speaking rather than about the mocha or squid. They are describing the speaker's attitude or opinion of these foods.

The point is that when statements are *subjectively* true, as Michael explained to Isaac, their truth depends on the attitude, opinion or belief system of the one speaking them. This does not mean they are any less important or not quite as true or anything of the sort. It just means that the speaking subject is the one who determines or creates the truth of the statement. When someone says "mochas are good," the statement is true only because that person likes mochas. For him or her, it's true that they are good. In fact, he or she is the one who makes the statement true.

This means, of course, that a conflicting statement, say, "mochas are *not* good," could also be true if it were uttered by another person who felt differently about those frothy drinks. Both statements, "mochas are good" and "mochas are not good," could be true. This is the nature of subjective statements.

Objectively true statements are different. Examples of these are "The Starbucks Coffee Company makes café mochas," and "President John F. Kennedy was assassinated in 1963." These statements do not merely give us information about the person speaking them, they tell us something about the Starbucks Coffee Company and the late U.S. president.

Furthermore, the truth of objective statements does not depend on the opinion or beliefs of the person who utters them. Rather, their truth is there to be *recognized* or *discovered* by someone, not *determined* or *created* by that person. If my friend disagrees with an objective statement I have made, I have no choice but to tell him that one of us is wrong. We can't both be correct. That is the nature of objective statements.

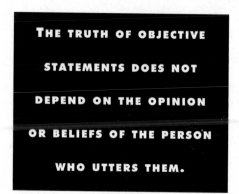

THE TRUTH OF OBJECTIVE STATEMENTS DOES NOT DEPEND ON THE OPINION OR BELIEFS OF THE PERSON WHO UTTERS THEM.

We all understand the difference between objective and subjective statements, and we work with them every day. It only becomes a problem when someone treats a subjective statement as though it were objective or vice versa, something logic textbooks refer to as the subjectivist fallacy.[9]

An example of this fallacy is treating your attitude toward mochas, squid or spinach as though it were something others should agree with you about or else they are just plain wrong: "I said spinach is good and it is good, and you're going to like it!" or "If you don't like this mocha, there's something wrong with you." When anything like this is said, we detect a problem even if we aren't able to give it a label.

In passing, it's worth noting that the distinction between subjective and objective is not always clear or easy to make. Beauty is a prime example. Is the beauty of the flowerbed in my front yard in my eyes only (subjective) or is it in the flowers themselves (objective)? If my neighbor and I disagree about whether my flowers are beautiful, does it mean that

---

[9]For a helpful explanation of the subjectivist fallacy, see Brooke Noel Moore and Richard Parker, *Critical Thinking* (Mountain View, Calif.: Mayfield Publishing, 2001), pp. 151-53. Moore and Parker are especially useful in that they provide examples both of this fallacy and of other statements that may appear to be cases of this fallacy but are not.

one of us must be wrong (beauty is objective) or that both of us could be correct (beauty is subjective), as in the case of squid or mochas? This difficulty doesn't mean that the categories of objective and subjective don't exist or that statements aren't one or the other, only that there are difficult cases in which it is hard to know whether a statement is objective or subjective.

The point of this distinction is that when the moral relativist asserts that there are no objectively true moral principles that apply to all people consistently, he or she is consigning all moral judgments to the subjective category. They are treated just like our statements about the way food tastes. Therefore moral judgments, from this perspective, don't refer to anything objective. We don't *recognize* or *discover* their truth as we do with objective statements. Rather, morality is a personal, private matter, and when we say "abortion is wrong" or "honesty is good," we really mean "we do not like abortion" and "we appreciate honesty." The highly significant implication of this is that, as Michael asserted above, conflicting moral judgments can both be true, just as conflicting statements about the way food tastes can be.[10]

Notice how this thinking is illustrated in the following interchange between three baseball umpires who were overheard discussing how they perform their jobs.

First umpire: I call 'em as I see 'em!

Second umpire: I call 'em as they are!

Third umpire: They ain't nuthin' till I call 'em.[11]

Leaving aside the first umpire's statement, which is open to more than one interpretation, consider the striking difference between the statements made by the second and third umpires. Here, the second umpire

---

[10]See William Frankena, *Ethics,* 2nd ed. (Englewood Cliffs, N.J.: Prentice-Hall, 1973), pp. 109-10 for a fuller description and analysis of various kinds of ethical relativism. See chapter two of Robert L. Holmes's *Basic Moral Philosophy* (Belmont, Calif.: Wadsworth, 1993), for another informative chapter on various elements of ethical relativism.

[11]This illustration is taken from Brian J. Walsh and J. Richard Middleton, *Truth Is Stranger Than It Used to Be* (Downers Grove, Ill.: InterVarsity Press, 1995), p. 31.

has a fully objective view of each pitch as it heads toward the batter. It is either a strike or ball, and he claims to be astute enough to call it what it is. The implication is that a different call would be wrong.

Not so with the third umpire. The ball is neither a strike nor a ball as it heads toward the batter—that is, until he calls it. His call determines what it is. If he yells "Strike!" then that is what the pitch becomes. The implication is that a different call would be just as correct if he so decided, since the pitch "ain't nuthin' " till he calls it.[12]

How is this relevant to moral relativism? The third umpire's thinking, when applied to morality, gives us moral relativism. Just as the third umpire didn't recognize any pitch as being a strike or ball on its way toward the batter, the moral relativist doesn't recognize any action as being objectively good or evil, whether it be honesty, respect, loyalty, abortion, extramarital sex, dishonesty or any other action. These may be morally right or wrong in your mind, but in a pluralistic culture like ours, others will regard them differently. We should respect others' views and not call them wrong just because they differ from ours since, in reality, neither of us is wrong. Both are right because the truth of moral judgments is subjective. It depends on and is determined by the individual person's opinion and belief system. Conflicting moral judgments can both be correct, and we have no right to impose our moral values on others. This was Michael's contention to Isaac.

But this results in moral confusion because at the same time as our society publicly avows this relativistic conception of morality, it is quite willing to roundly condemn the very things it opposes, things like intolerance, the imposition of one's moral views on others, bigotry, child abuse, violations of the rights of women, the treatment of workers in sweatshops in Third World countries, environmental and animal abuse and so on.

This is confusion because moral relativism undercuts the basis for such condemnations. As much as relativists may want to, they simply cannot condemn intolerance, bigotry, rape, slavery or anything else for

---

[12]Ibid.

the simple reason that these are not objectively wrong. If morality is purely subjective, personal and private, as they affirm, then the most they can say about actions like these is that they offend their *personal taste*. They don't like them. They have a bad feeling or attitude toward them and would not choose them for themselves. But if moral relativism is true, they must accept that others obviously have different moral tastes that they are equally entitled to call legitimate and good. Moral relativists simply have no right to impose their moral tastes on other people. But, of course, most moral relativists go right on spiritedly condemning the actions they themselves oppose.

The confusion doesn't end here. It goes deeper because not only do most moral relativists *condemn* actions they oppose, they are also in the business of *commending* the activities they approve of. Respect for others, honesty, compassion, service to one's community, self-sacrifice and going the second mile are widely commended across our culture, in some cases with official awards. Witness the deep approval of those who risked their own lives trying to save the lives of Jewish people during the Holocaust.

But again, moral commendation has no place if morality is purely relative. No action would be objectively good or evil. It's just that certain actions appeal to your or my personal moral tastes while others don't. These, of course, vary from person to person, and from the subjectivist's point of view, this kind of commendation would amount to commending people for having the same moral tastes as I do. This would be as absurd as commending people for having the same tastes in food as I do. I may be happy about this; it makes it possible for us to enjoy meals together, but I wouldn't commend them morally for sharing my tastes in food or for satisfying these tastes. But again, most relativists carry on commending the actions they approve of along with their condemnations of those they oppose.

It becomes clear that there are very few true practicing moral relativists around. Our actions betray our true convictions. While we *say* morality is subjective, we *act* as though it is objectively real. Few of us manage to escape the notion that certain things are truly good while others are genuinely evil. It looks as though we will have to decide. Will we be moral relativists, as so many claim to be, or will we carry on commending and condemning various activities, attitudes and characteristics, as we so readily do? Doing both leads to a fundamental confusion.

My own observation is that the place to begin in moving beyond this confusing state of affairs is to recognize that, whatever we may say of ourselves, our actions betray our real convictions. They tell the real story of what we believe, and virtually none of us succeed in living as true moral relativists. We recognize the existence and the foundational importance of objective moral truth in our day-to-day experience. If we are not actually moral relativists after all, then the way forward is to recognize and declare this fact and leave moral relativism behind explicitly—as our actions show we are already doing implicitly.

REAL MORAL DISAGREEMENT ASSUMES THE EXISTENCE OF OBJECTIVE GOOD AND EVIL.

Our actions tell an even deeper story about our true convictions. A quick examination of our own behavior reveals that not only do *we* recognize objective moral good and evil when we see it, we expect *others* to recognize these as well—and they do, which is why they make excuses for acting rudely, dishonestly or abusively when they would never make similar excuses for treating others honestly, fairly or kindly.

Even the fact that we disagree about the morality of certain controversial actions doesn't change the fact that we recognize the existence of objective good and evil. In fact, as strange as it may sound, real moral disagreement assumes the existence of objective good and evil. If there weren't some objective moral standard that both people really agree on, there would be nothing to disagree over, just as there is nothing to disagree about in the way food tastes. All of our conflicting views would be right. But we are convinced they are not all right, which is why we disagree.

C. S. Lewis, in fact, points to this phenomenon of moral disagreement, which he calls quarreling, as the sure-fire proof that we all recognize the existence of a law of human nature, his term for an objective moral standard. He invites us to observe precisely how people quarrel, and then draws out the underlying assumption necessarily in the minds of both quarreling parties. Without it, no genuine human quarreling could take place:

> Everyone has heard people quarrelling. Sometimes it sounds funny and sometimes it sounds merely unpleasant. . . . They say things like this: "How'd you like it if anyone did the same to you?"—"That's my seat, I was there first"—"Leave him alone, he isn't doing you any harm." . . . "Come on, you promised." Now what interests me about all these remarks is that the man who makes them is not merely saying that the other man's behaviour does not happen to please him. He is appealing to some kind of standard of behaviour which he expects the other man to know about. And the other man very seldom replies: "To hell with your standard." Nearly always he tries to make out that what he has been doing does not really go against the standard, or that if it does there is some special excuse. . . . It looks very much as if both parties had in mind some kind of Law or Rule of fair play or decent behaviour or morality . . . about which they really agreed. And they have. If they had not, they . . . could not *quarrel* in the human sense of the word. Quarrelling means trying to show that the other man is in the wrong. And there would be no sense in trying to do that unless you and he had some sort of agreement as to what Right and Wrong are.[13]

It's hard to deny that we recognize the existence of objective moral truth. In fact, we recognize it so strongly that we have developed special terms to refer to the occasional person who doesn't seem to recognize it. We label them psychopaths because we believe something important is missing in such people. Even though they don't recognize that it's better

---

[13]C. S. Lewis, *Mere Christianity* (New York: Macmillan, 1952), pp. 17-18.

to be honest, respectful or tolerant than dishonest, rude and intolerant, they should.

And here we have what is perhaps the most reliable proof of all that most members of our society do indeed recognize the existence of objective moral truth, namely, our commitment to principles such as tolerance. It has become, in effect, Western society's supreme virtue. At least this one principle is consistently held to be good. It is, in other words, treated as an objective virtue, one that ought not be set aside at will. It is the standard by which we judge our actions, words, attitudes, organizations, policies and most other human endeavors. As we interact with others along the way, we never get far before encountering this moral principle. Those who demonstrate it are commended while those who don't are immediately castigated, even marginalized. Tolerance is occasionally used as a sledgehammer to pressure people to act or think in ways we want them to. And it is an effective sledgehammer indeed. After all, who wants to be labeled intolerant?

But what, exactly, is tolerance? Is it as good as our society has come to think? And how should we understand this concept or have fruitful discussions with others about it? Few concepts have caused as much confusion as this one, and we must address it.

5

WHAT IS TRUTH?

Tolerance and Truth
in an Age of Pluralism

"I want the truth!"

"You can't handle the truth!"

**TOM CRUISE AND JACK NICHOLSON
IN *A FEW GOOD MEN***

"Intolerance is a great evil."

TALK RADIO PROGRAMS

"Zero tolerance for deadbeat dads!"

BUMPER STICKERS AND BILLBOARDS

Something striking has happened to the concepts of truth, tolerance and pluralism in Western culture. Talk shows wrangle over them, newspaper editorialists pontificate on them, lecturers seek to elucidate them. Meanwhile the rest of us appeal to them on every imaginable question, whether to stake out the moral high ground for ourselves or to browbeat someone who disagrees with us. These concepts have become cultural staples, yet for many of us they have also become too hot to handle. Somehow they have been transformed into fighting words that can raise the temperature in a room, often touching a raw nerve by their very mention.

What is more, there is little consensus on the proper definitions or uses of these concepts in the first place. What is truth, really? And what constitutes tolerance or intolerance for that matter? Is tolerance always good and intolerance always bad? Should we be happy or concerned that Western culture is pluralistic? All of these questions receive vastly different answers from the people we rub shoulders with, and the challenge for any of us wishing to engage our culture on issues that matter is clear: How can we enter into discussion of these hot-button concepts without things turning ugly? Given our confused and heated environment, is there any realistic hope of doing so?

Consider the dramatically different responses we can expect if we decide to plunge in. Some people consider terms like *truth* and *tolerance* too problematic to even use, preferring to use other terms instead. How do we get started discussing truth or tolerance with someone who will not even use these words? Others go further and regard these concepts as actually dangerous, the root cause of serious social ills in our world, and choose to reject them altogether.

When it comes to the concept of pluralism, many people celebrate this phenomenon, arguing that the diversity it has brought has made us all richer. Others, however, far from regarding this as a healthy development for Western culture, believe it has signaled a perilous loss of consensus that can only lead to an erosion of social and moral cohesion. Who is right? As even the historian Stephen Stein declared a few years ago when writing about the effects of pluralism on Western culture, "the time-honored concepts [that previously provided cultural cohesion] are [now] inadequate for the task at hand."[1] Indeed, would anyone deny that the reality of pluralism sometimes makes us wonder whether there is such a thing as American or Canadian or

---

[1]Stephen J. Stein, "Something Old, Something New, Something Borrowed, Something Left to Do: Choosing a Textbook for Religion in America," *Religion and American Culture* 3 (1993): 226.

British society any more. Or is there really only a great agglomeration of subcultures coexisting side by side with different visions of what is good and bad?[2]

We debate these concepts passionately and apply them to virtually every issue that matters to us. But do we understand them? Unfortunately, it seems to me at least, that while there has been plenty of fervor and zeal about these critical ideas, clarity has been in short supply. Notice the way Michael reacts to a local newspaper editorial that he considers to be especially narrow and intolerant:

Michael (waving a newspaper): Can you believe this intolerance? How disgusting! Why can't these people mind their own business?

Isaac: What people?

Michael: People like the person who wrote this editorial. They're always sounding off about some issue, telling the rest of us what is good for us. If it's not sex or marijuana, it's stem-cell research or cloning, as in this article.

Isaac: Oh, those people.

Michael: If they don't agree with what the rest of us are doing, why can't they just let it go? It's not bothering them. They don't have to do it. I don't know about you, but I want to live in a world that is tolerant.

Isaac: Now there's a firebrand word. Do you mean tolerance toward everything?

Michael: Well, we can't pick and choose what we'll be tolerant toward, can we? As soon as that starts, we'll have lost the whole point of tolerance. Who gets to do the picking and choosing? I just have no use for intolerance or intolerant people.

---

[2]For a wider discussion of contemporary social attitudes toward pluralism, see William R. Hutchinson, *Religious Pluralism in America: The Contentious History of a Founding Ideal* (New Haven, Conn.: Yale University Press, 2003), pp. 1-9, 219-40. Other chapters in this text address historical attitudes toward pluralism as it has developed in America.

Isaac: Can you tolerate them?

Michael: Very funny!

Isaac: What do you mean by tolerance?

Michael: I mean accepting other people and their viewpoints. That's the problem with this editorial. The person who wrote it obviously doesn't accept any viewpoint but his own. He's right, and everyone else is wrong. How intolerant!

Isaac: Well, I happen to believe some viewpoints are true and others are false.

Michael: You sound like the guy who wrote this article.

Isaac: Now *that* is funny. Are you calling me intolerant?

Michael: If the shoe fits, wear it. This guy thinks his views are true, and he's implying all the way through that anyone who disagrees with him is wrong. He even uses the word *false* here.

Isaac: So your problem is with truth. Is that it?

Michael: My problem is with people who think their views are the only ones that are true and that people who disagree with them are false.

Isaac: So your problem is with *objective* truth.

Michael: Now there's a term I make a practice of staying away from. For one thing, there's no basis for thinking one has objective truth since we all see the world and what we take to be true through our own perspectives. We all have glasses given to us by our communities, and we can't help but view the world through them.

Isaac: We do?

Michael: Yes. The world looks the way it does to us because of our glasses. Truth is actually something constructed by our communities, and it changes from one community to another.

Isaac: Hey, wait just a minute. Last time we talked, you told me it was *people* who determined the truth of moral statements, not *communities*.

Michael: That's true too. It's just that behind every person's idea of what is true and false is a community that has given her the glasses through which she sees the world. Of course we all *think* our ideas are true. They seem true to us, but other people have different ideas given to them by their communities, which seem just as right to them. None of these ideas are *objectively* true, as you say.

Isaac: So truth is something that is constructed by my community?

Michael: Absolutely! But it's worse than that. Objective truth is also a dangerous idea.

Isaac: Dangerous? Wow, that's a serious accusation.

Michael: I agree, but people who talk about objective truth scare me.

Isaac: *Scare you?* Aren't we becoming overly dramatic?

Michael: Not at all. That kind of talk about *objective* truth leads to all sorts of intolerant behavior. It makes people say things like, "I'm right, you're wrong, because I have *the truth.*" We would be better off if we rejected that kind of truth and chose tolerance instead. In a pluralistic society like ours, other people have different views than we do, and we've got to accept them.

Isaac: So it's tolerance *versus* truth?

Michael: I couldn't have said it better myself.

Isaac: Some things bother me about what you're saying.

Michael: Why am I not surprised? What things?

Isaac: You just said *tolerance* means accepting other people and their viewpoints.

Michael: Yes.

Isaac: But it doesn't sound like you are accepting the viewpoint of the person who wrote this editorial. After all, he is only expressing his view.

Michael: Trust you to stick up for the person who wrote this.

Isaac: It looks like you tolerate everything but intolerance.

Michael: Very funny. What's that supposed to mean?

Isaac: You said the editorialist is intolerant because he doesn't accept other people's viewpoints.

Michael: He certainly is.

Isaac: Well, at the risk of repeating myself, it doesn't sound to me like you're accepting *his* viewpoint. In fact, you're making it sound like your view on tolerance is true and his view is false. How intolerant of you, Michael.

Michael (growing irritated): You're calling *me* intolerant?

Isaac: I think *you* just called yourself intolerant.

Michael: Ooh! I see we're moving to a whole new level here.

Isaac: And there's something else.

Michael: What now?

Isaac: Those billboards and bumper stickers. You know the ones. Big bold letters: "Zero Tolerance of Child Abuse" or ". . . Drug Trafficking" or ". . . Deadbeat Dads." They make it sound like there are some things we shouldn't tolerate.

Michael (quickly flipping back to the newspaper): Hey, wait a minute! That's in this editorial too.

Isaac: You don't say.

Michael (scanning to the end of the editorial to the writer's initials): Are you telling me . . . ?

Isaac: Yes, it's true. They asked for guest editorials this week, and I had some time before exams.

Michael (shaking his head): I might have known. Boy, have we got some talking to do!

Isaac: I think your glasses are different from mine.

Michael and Isaac have raised a few of the issues that enter into discussions surrounding tolerance and truth in a pluralistic society. Unfortunately, as they demonstrated in their discussion, confusion is often the order of the day in conversations about these ideas. I have often begun public lectures on truth and tolerance by asking a number of diagnostic questions. My purpose in asking them is to help audience members probe their own minds to determine what they presently think about these concepts. If confusion exists, the first step must be to know it is there. Only then can we hope to untangle it. The questions are these:

1. On a scale of 1-10, how important is truth to you?

2. Using the same scale, how important is tolerance to you?

3. In your opinion, are these problematic terms?

4. Do you believe people of faith should think differently about truth and tolerance than others do?

5. Do you hope people will treat you in a manner that is both truthful and tolerant?

I have always been intrigued by a few of the responses from audiences. Although a majority of those present usually answer yes to question three, indicating a widespread feeling that these concepts are unclear or problematic in some way, virtually all, so far, have also answered with an emphatic yes to question five. How can this be? If we think the terms *truth* and *tolerance* are unclear, how can we be so sure we want others to treat us in these ways? My own conclusion is that however problematic we may think these concepts are, most of us obviously feel we have a clear enough idea of what they mean to forcefully declare our wish to be treated both truthfully and with tolerance.

I suspect, however, that some of us may wish to avoid any discussion of truth and tolerance altogether, and of course it is always possible to avoid *talking* about these ideas. What we can't avoid is *thinking* about them. We simply can't get far in any normal day without assuming and implicitly believing something about both of these terms. If I absent-mindedly walk to the wrong car in the shopping mall parking lot and try to insert my keys into the door (unfortunately, not a far-fetched example in my case), I'm liable to hear a very determined voice behind me saying, "Excuse me, that's not your car. It's mine!" I can assure you that at that moment both the person speaking and I are assuming something very definite about both truth and tolerance. He will be placing great importance on the truth of the matter without it ever occurring to him that he might need to explain to me his understanding of the concept of truth. I, on the other hand, will hope for tolerance, while at the same time finding myself unable to avoid the embarrassing truth he is putting before me.

And this is how it is for most of our day-to-day activities. The ideas of truth and tolerance are simply too closely connected to most of what we say and do for any of us to avoid acting or speaking on the basis of some assumed understanding of them. Furthermore, this is true whether or not we ever actually put into words what we think about these ideas. In our nonphilosophical moments, our statements, actions and reactions tell the real story of what we think about them.

But how *should* we think about truth and tolerance? Why have they become such important buzzwords in Western culture? Should we seek them or shun them? One thing is sure: our understanding of these concepts will directly influence the way we live and interact with others.

PLURALISM: AN UNDENIABLE REALITY

Western society has become thoroughly pluralistic. That is the first thing we must recognize when trying to understand our passionate attitudes toward both truth and tolerance. It's also worth noting that this is not true of every society or culture in the world, and some of us may wish it were not true where we live. We may favor a society in which one worldview (preferably our own) was dominant and others were accorded a lesser status. We may believe that this sort of society would be superior to a pluralistic one. However, in North America and Western Europe at least, anyone who believes this will find that even this very belief will, at best, be regarded as simply one view among others; at worst it will be shunned as unacceptable. That is the reality of pluralism, which permeates Western society.

Furthermore, Western governments virtually guarantee the current state of affairs by opening the doors to immigrants from around the world. More importantly, they also grant all citizens protection under the law to believe and live by any ideology they wish, within certain limitations.

What does it mean that a particular culture is pluralistic? Put simply it means that within that culture there is a large menu of worldview and faith options coexisting side by side, with none being truly dominant. This is certainly the case in Western societies. The major world religions such as Christianity, Islam, Buddhism, Hinduism, Sikhism all have strong followings, as do many of the sects that have broken from them over the years. Then there are nonreligious ideologies such as naturalism, socialism, Marxism, humanism and atheism, which also have adherents.

These followers of different worldviews give different answers to the fundamental questions of life: Is there a God? If so, how can a person come to know a being like this? Where did human beings come from? What is the true nature of humanity? Is there an afterlife? What is the nature of truth? Is the supernatural possible, or is nature all there is? What is good, and how can we discover it?[3]

---

[3]For a description of worldviews, as well as tools for analyzing them, see Brian J. Walsh and J. Richard Middleton, *The Transforming Vision* (Downers Grove, Ill.: InterVarsity Press, 1984), especially pp. 15-39. See also James Sire, *The Universe Next Door,* 4th ed. (Downers Grove, Ill.: InterVarsity Press, 2004).

These different worldviews also produce clashing moral perspectives on what should be tolerated within culture. The question of same-sex marriage is one particularly vexing example. While an increasing number of citizens not only tolerate but actually approve, even celebrate, such marriages, at the same time a substantial group remains staunchly opposed, preferring an outright ban on them.

Other examples could be cited as well. Are we, as a culture, willing to tolerate vulgar, offensive and insulting language on our airwaves, or should we revoke the license of any station guilty of such vulgarity? "If you don't like it, just turn the dial!" we are chided by the proponents of broadcast freedom. "The people must be free to decide, and the ratings will tell us their decision." And if those ratings are to be trusted, these proponents are in good company. Station owner Patrice Demers, of CHOI-FM in Quebec City, Quebec, bought a money-losing station in 1996, and using the lewd and crude format, he brought its ratings up from last place to first, gaining an audience of hundreds of thousands of people. During the same period however, the number of complaints also rose considerably. The Canadian regulatory commission considered the base level of discussion unfit for public consumption, and the station's license was revoked.[4]

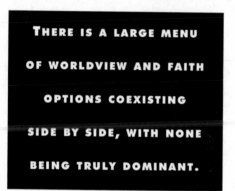

THERE IS A LARGE MENU OF WORLDVIEW AND FAITH OPTIONS COEXISTING SIDE BY SIDE, WITH NONE BEING TRULY DOMINANT.

This pluralistic reality forces us to consider a number of questions about truth and tolerance. Why has tolerance been elevated to such a prominent position in this kind of society? What is tolerance in the first place, and what is its relationship with truth? Are tolerance and truth

---

[4]This story was reported in one of Canada's national newspapers, *The Globe and Mail,* July 14, 2004, pp. A1, A6. Since the story was first reported the decision to revoke the station's license has been challenged in court, and at the time of this writing the case is still in court.

compatible, or do we have to choose between them, as Michael seemed to believe? How important is the concept of truth? Could we dispense with it? *Should* we dispense with it in the interests of promoting tolerance and pluralism? Could it actually be a dangerous concept that threatens the peace in a diverse society? These questions require clear thinking.

TOLERANCE: THE NEW BUZZWORD

You've probably noticed that, in our contemporary culture, few terms are more potent than *tolerance*. "You are intolerant!" is one of the most stinging rebukes leveled at a person. We have only to listen to a few talk-radio shows or read a handful of newspaper editorials to see that tolerance has been exalted nearly to the position of the supreme cultural virtue. If an idea, viewpoint or person is deemed to be intolerant, they are immediately treated with contempt. They have violated the cardinal cultural virtue. How has tolerance come to possess this lofty status?

In *The Closing of the American Mind,* professor Alan Bloom makes a highly significant assertion that helps answer this question. He contends that there is one thing most every university professor in America can be nearly certain of, and that is that when students arrive at their classrooms, virtually all will believe and simply assume that objective truth does not exist. In fact, the students are so sure of themselves about this that many express genuine shock when this assumption is challenged or even questioned.[5]

The incoming students typically believe that you can have your truth, I can have mine, and if our truths differ or even conflict, it doesn't matter. Truth is not seen as an objective, universal entity, existing independently of individuals. Rather, it is viewed as something personal, private and subjective, connected to individuals, even determined by them, like the third umpire in the previous chapter (they ain't nuthin' till I call 'em).

Since Bloom wrote those words, and with the rise of postmodernism, truth has increasingly come to be viewed as something tied not only to individuals but also to communities. As Michael explained to Isaac,

---

[5]Alan Bloom, *The Closing of the American Mind* (New York: Simon & Schuster, 1987), pp. 25-26.

truth is regarded as the expression of a specific community. Not only our specific beliefs about what is true but also our very understanding of the concept of truth itself is rooted in the community we belong to. This is a corporate understanding of truth, and it makes truth relative to the community in which a person participates. The ideas we hold to be true are true only for our communities. They are our truths, and as there are many different communities, there are also many different truths.[6]

This understanding of truth has had a powerful impact on the way many in our culture have come to regard not only truth but tolerance as well. Bloom went on to observe that for students who regard truth subjectively, the idea of objective truth—independent of individuals and of which we try to discover and learn—is considered a dangerous idea. Why? Because it leads people to claim and genuinely believe that they are right and others are wrong. This attitude is viewed as the cause of terrible ills in our world: wars, riots, intolerance, bigotry, racism and violence. The new goal, therefore, is not to seek truth so we can reject what is false but rather to get rid of the very idea of truth altogether. Instead, we should be tolerant toward all points of view, to regard all views as roughly equal.

TRUTH VERSUS TOLERANCE

Notice what has happened in this reasoning? Truth has been identified as the culprit, the cause of many of the world's greatest evils. It isn't any particular truths that are held to be guilty. Rather, the very notion of truth itself is wrong-headed.

This thinking has developed because truth has been set in opposition to tolerance, and tolerance has come to be regarded as the way for people of differing ideologies and faiths to live side by side peacefully. The more we accept the views of other people as roughly equal with our own, the more harmoniously we will be able to live together. Truth, on the other hand, allegedly provides a basis for exclusivism, divisiveness, marginalization and violence. The existence of truth itself is thought to be what generates and sustains these ills. If there were no truth, there would be

---

[6]For a further explanation of a postmodern understanding of truth, see Stan Grenz, *Primer on Postmodernism* (Grand Rapids: Eerdmans, 1996), pp. 5-15.

no basis for excluding certain views as untrue or for marginalizing certain groups of people who embrace ideas we believe to be wrong.

If this is the case, of course, it means that we have to choose between truth and tolerance. We can't embrace both. Believing in objective truth, according to this view, produces intolerance. So we must choose. Truth or tolerance.

What are we to make of this line of reasoning? Must we abandon real, objective truth as a dangerous enemy? Should we regard truth as a strictly private, subjective and relative entity in order to be tolerant of others?

This is a pressing question, and honesty compels us not to miss the important insight that we do, in fact, see and interpret the world through a set of tinted glasses given to us by our respective communities. The framework of our thought and the assumptions behind our views (of which we are usually unaware) are seldom the result of personal reflection and discovery. Our communities provided them for us lock, stock and barrel. If our communities were different, our tinted glasses would also be different, and consequently our interpretations of reality and what we take to be true would be different as well. But does this mean objective truth is unattainable and we should reject it altogether, embracing tolerance instead?

If we do, we've moved too quickly in accepting this extreme conclusion. The immediate problem for anyone trying to reject objective truth is that it just doesn't go away very easily. In fact, the very act of denying objective truth involves us in a self-refuting and ultimately frustrating exercise—the person who asserts that objective truth does not exist or that it is unattainable believes that both these statements are objectively true. In making them, the person refutes him- or herself. The dilemma for such a person lies in the question, Is it really true that there is no objective truth?

Likewise, those who assert that (1) there is no objective or universal truth, but (2) all truth is a communal construct that varies from community to community, believe these very assertions about the nature of truth are objectively true for all communities. This is the way truth is for all people everywhere. Again, in the very act of denying universal, objective truth, this statement affirms at least one objective truth.

Michael encountered this self-reference problem when he emphatically declared the author of the editorial to be wrong while at the same time describing truth as a relative entity. If it is relative as he claimed, then he had no basis for calling this author's statement genuinely wrong. The most he could say is that this writer's statement did not fit with his view of truth. But the writer's view deserved to be treated equally with his own.

There is more. People who reject objective truth often do so because of certain beliefs or convictions that lead them to feel they must reject it—we ought to accept others who are different than us; we shouldn't discriminate against them or go to war with them. But aren't these underlying beliefs held to be objectively true? That is why they aren't free to ignore or set them aside. How then can they continue to reject objective truth?

Where does this leave us? Does the undeniable existence of real, objective truth force us to be intolerant? Are tolerance and truth incompatible? Do we have to choose between them? I don't think we can resolve this question without first answering a more fundamental one, namely, What is true tolerance? A lack of clarity about the meaning of *tolerance* will prevent us from knowing whether or not it is compatible with truth.

WHAT IS TRUE TOLERANCE?

In contemporary North American culture, tolerance has come to be virtually synonymous with agreement. The way to be tolerant toward an idea or practice is to agree with it, or better yet to affirm it, possibly even to celebrate it. And the further we move on this scale from agreement to affirmation to celebration, the more tolerant we are. This view of tolerance becomes evident when people speak out against certain viewpoints or practices. They are often immediately labeled intolerant for doing nothing more than voicing their disagreement. In other words, stating reasons for disagreeing with a view constitutes intolerance.

But does disagreement with a viewpoint or practice really constitute intolerance? Put another way, do we demonstrate our tolerance of a certain point of view by agreeing with it? If we reflect briefly on the notion of tolerance, it becomes clear that something has gone wrong with our understanding of it. Tolerance does not require agreement. It couldn't possibly require it. In fact, as odd as it may sound to us who have been conditioned by the recent common usage of this term, the very idea of tolerance actually entails *disagreement.* To see this, consider the obvious fact that if I agree with a certain idea, I hardly need to tolerate that idea since I already agree with it. It makes no sense to talk about tolerating things I already agree with. The very notion is humorous.

What then is tolerance? It is an attitude that says, "I disagree with something you are saying or doing. I wish you would stop, but I still accept your right to say or do the thing I disagree with." A person demonstrating this attitude might go so far as to defend the right of another person to do something he or she finds disagreeable. But notice, none of this implies agreement. In fact, it presupposes that one person *disagrees* with what another person is doing or saying. Otherwise the question of whether or not to tolerate it would never arise.

What does this mean for truth and tolerance? If I am correct in this analysis, it means truth and tolerance are not opposing concepts at all. On the contrary, they are complementary and may even need each other for the simple reason that without different points of view (that is, disagreement about what is true or right), the need for tolerance doesn't arise. And the reality is that people (group A) living in a pluralistic society will soon encounter others (group B) who are convinced that the things group A thinks are true are not true at all, and the ways group A thinks things should be done are not the ways we (groups A and B) should do them. It is in these moments that we are presented with opportunities to show tolerance. The deeper the disagreement, the more difficult it will be to demonstrate tolerance, but it is only when the disagreement is real and serious that true, meaningful tolerance is demonstrated. When the difference of opinion is shallow and of no serious significance to a person or group, tolerance is easy.

SHOULD I BE TOLERANT?

This brings us to the most important question of all: should I be tolerant? The initial answer must be yes for at least three reasons. First, by demonstrating a tolerant attitude we show respect for the dignity of others, especially those we disagree with. Our very action implies that, however strongly we may disagree with them, they are rational human beings who have something worthwhile to contribute.

Second, in the very act of showing tolerance and of welcoming the expression of viewpoints we disagree with, there is an implied recognition of our own fallibility as humans. We don't have all knowledge on every issue, and we know it. At the best of times our perspectives are limited, and we sometimes get things wrong. But if so, then hearing and evaluating contrasting opinions makes eminent sense, and that cannot happen if we summarily squash the expression of ideas and practices we disagree with.

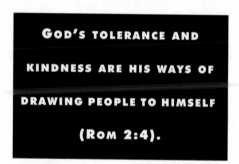

GOD'S TOLERANCE AND KINDNESS ARE HIS WAYS OF DRAWING PEOPLE TO HIMSELF (ROM 2:4).

Third, we do ourselves a serious disservice by not hearing opinions we disagree with. Not only might the opposing opinion actually be right and ours wrong, but even if not, as British philosopher John Stuart Mill pointed out in the nineteenth century, a wrong opinion may, and often does, contain a piece of the truth or some other insight we would miss if the opinion were not expressed.[7] Furthermore, argued Mill, even if the other opinion is wrong through and through, there is much to be gained from having to defend truth in the face of error. This very exercise prevents truth from collapsing into dead orthodoxy. Both our *understanding* of the truth and the *grounds* for it become weak if we are never called on to defend it.

---

[7]John Stuart Mill, *On Liberty and Other Essays,* ed. John Gray (Oxford: Oxford University Press, n.d.), pp. 59-60.

It is worth noting that Christianity not only calls for tolerance but also instructs us to go beyond this and actually "love our enemies." Jesus himself gave this moral instruction. What is more, God himself is said to be tolerant. While disapproving of certain actions of people, he nonetheless grants us the freedom to do some things he disapproves of. As the apostle Paul put it, God's tolerance and kindness are his ways of drawing people to himself (Rom 2:4). No one ever became a genuine follower of Jesus through coercion.

The only remaining question is whether we should tolerate *everything* people say or do. That is the question Isaac put to Michael early in the dialogue. Notwithstanding the fact that Michael confidently implied we should, it takes very little thought to see that we should do no such thing. Michael spoke too soon, as do some others in conversations on tolerance. We rightly proclaim zero tolerance against drinking and driving, child abuse, drug trafficking, terrorism, theft, rape, attacks on women and a host of other clearly hurtful actions. We do so because we've learned that this is the way to protect what we deeply value in society. We've learned that women are safer in a society that does not tolerate attacks on them, that children are safer in a world where there is no tolerance for child abuse and that we are all safer when our society doesn't tolerate a cavalier attitude toward life itself.

The point is simply that the fundamental goods in society, treasures we hold dear and never want to lose, like justice, safety, liberty and life itself, are protected by an intolerance of their opposites.

WHAT THEN SHOULD WE DO?

If we believe in objective truth and tolerance, what can we do? Let me summarize with three affirmations.

1. *Speak the truth in love.* This is a biblical directive that implies both that there is real truth and that we should seek it and speak it with an attitude of compassion. This directive brings attitudes of arrogance and bigotry to an end. Rather than trying to reject the concept of objective truth, which we've seen is impossible to do, we ought to rec-

ognize the community's influence on our views of what is true and exercise a deep-seated humility in the way we hold our personal interpretations of the world around us.

2. ***Accept and respect the rights of others to do the same.*** This affirmation, taken together with the first one, has the great benefit of encouraging respectful dialogue with others of different persuasions. Following it will provide opportunities to welcome others to express their views, however different and conflicting with ours. Through this process we can all critique and learn from each other and hopefully draw closer to the truth.

3. ***Protect the treasures we value deeply by a legitimate intolerance toward their opposites.*** This is a simple recognition that as important as tolerance is, there is also a proper place for intolerance. In fact, it is deeply necessary in certain situations since it is our way of protecting what we hold dear and never want to lose. We protect treasures like justice, liberty, safety and life by refusing to tolerate violations of them.

6

KEEP YOUR MORALS TO YOURSELF

You Shall Not Impose

A number of years ago I was involved in a series of debates on six major university campuses across Canada. The topic was the moral permissibility of physician-assisted suicide. In the months preceding the debate I had spent many hours researching this moral question and had come prepared to debate the merits of changing public policy to legalize this practice. Many issues had to be considered:

- Did our respect for human dignity and individual autonomy require that we give people the choice to end their lives with a physician's help?

- Would it be better to legalize a practice that was happening anyway, sometimes with terrible consequences, in order to bring it out into the open where we could regulate it and make it more humane?

- Could legalization of this practice lead to a dangerously unstoppable, slippery-slope—ending in practices that most of us would find objectionable?

- Would legalization of this practice endanger our most vulnerable citizens, the elderly, terminally ill and disabled by putting them in a position where their own continued existence would become a choice they must make, and this at a time when they already feel they are a burden to others?

• Could the legalization of this practice result in a new kind of discrimination, namely, our picking and choosing which lives we would allow to die in the name of "death with dignity" (presumably the elderly, disabled and terminally ill), and which we would fight for (the young and able-bodied, some of whom also find life unbearable and want to die) even if it meant overriding their personal autonomy?

These and other issues like them were what I came prepared to deliberate. They were indeed raised, but my opponent raised another entirely different argument as well. This came as something of a surprise to me. The unexpected argument was that since I spoke from an overall religious perspective, my view on this moral issue was obviously a religious view. Therefore, I simply had no right to impose my view onto others who were not religious. It was an attempt to undercut my entire position in one fell swoop.

We've all probably heard the challenge: "You have no right to impose your moral values onto others. If you want to live by your own moral views, go ahead—it's a free country—but don't try to force them on anyone else." This is a common rebuke in Western society, and the person making it is usually very sincere, looking you squarely in the eyes. No one gets far in any discussion of moral issues without encountering this reprimand.

What are we to make of it? How should we respond when we hear this challenge? On one hand, it seems patently obvious that in a free society all people ought to be allowed to choose and hold their own moral opinions without feeling pressured into them. Others have a right to agree or disagree with our opinions, but they certainly have no right to force their own moral opinions onto us. That much is clear.

What is not so clear, however, is precisely what is meant by this challenge not to impose. How exactly does one commit or for that matter avoid the action being challenged? What does it mean to impose one's values onto others? This is not an easy question, and the lack of clarity creates confusion for anyone attempting to respond to this admonition.

Imagine the following discussion between Isaac, who is very willing to express his moral convictions on any issue, and Michael, who feels Isaac is far too outspoken about them.

Michael: You're at it again! Didn't you just hear yourself? You just can't help yourself can you!

Isaac: At what again? What did I do?

Michael (shaking his head): You were imposing your moral values on those people you were just talking to.

Isaac: I was?

Michael: Yes. You went from one issue to the next. Euthanasia. Cloning. Stem cells. Abortion. Sweatshops. I heard them all.

Isaac: Those are important issues, and we need to figure out what's right and wrong about them.

Michael: It's OK to have views about what's right and wrong on these issues, but sooner or later you're going to have to realize that your moral views are just that, *your* morals, not everyone else's. You have no right to impose them on others.

Isaac: Impose them on others? How did I do that?

Michael: You were spouting off your views on all those controversial issues, pretty dogmatically I might add.

Isaac: Sure, I was expressing my moral opinions. Don't you ever do that?

Michael: You were doing more than that. You were forgetting everything we've talked about before and were implying that if other people don't agree with your moral values, they are wrong. You might as well have come right out and said, "The rest of you should live according to my moral views." People like you scare me. You believe your views are the only right ones, and you try to push them onto the rest of us who don't agree with your views.

Isaac: Of course I believe my opinions are right; otherwise they wouldn't be my opinions. I thought we had a right to express our views. Don't you believe in individual liberty?

Michael: Yes, which is why I want to stop people like you from imposing your morals on the rest of us. It limits our rights and freedoms.

Isaac: Imposing my morals on the rest of you? Limiting your freedoms? Hmm, I'm going to have to figure out what that means.

Isaac is not the only one who will have to figure this out. Most of us would do well to stop and decipher what it means to impose our morals on other people. In the name of individual liberty Michael insisted that Isaac had no right to do this. This challenge to Isaac is interesting as much for what it does *not* do as for what it does. While challenging Isaac's right to impose his opinions on others, whatever that means, Michael made no attempt whatsoever to convince Isaac that his moral opinions were wrong or faulty. The rightness or wrongness of his viewpoints was simply not at issue in Michael's rebuke.

This is interesting since it is not our normal way of challenging particular moral views. We usually do so by trying to show that the moral view in question is mistaken, that a different view is better or closer to the truth or more in keeping with other things we believe. But things are different with this challenge. Rather than telling Isaac any of these things, Michael simply tells him he shouldn't force his moral views onto other people, and the reason he shouldn't is that they are *his personal moral views,* and he should keep them that way.

This challenge tends to be especially common if the person holding the moral views is perceived to hold them for religious reasons. If a woman who is thought to be a religious person is opposed to the use of human embryos for stem-cell research, for example, she will probably be told that her view on this issue is a religious view because she obviously holds it for religious reasons. After all, she is a religious person, but because many other people in our society don't hold her religious perspectives, she has no right to impose her religious-moral views on them. In other words, it has now become an issue of individual liberty, even religious liberty.

We should never underestimate the power of this challenge in our culture. Indeed, it has the effect of marginalizing or delegitimizing entire viewpoints. The practical result of telling someone her viewpoint on a particular issue must not be imposed on others is to push that viewpoint into a corner where it is no longer given the right even to be heard, and this happens without a reason or argument expressed as to what is wrong with the view being marginalized. No argument is deemed necessary since the viewpoints are regarded as religious viewpoints, and that is all that is necessary since others around us are not religious. These viewpoints are simply irrelevant to them and shouldn't be "imposed on them."

> **EVERY LAW REFLECTS SOMEONE'S IDEAS OF RIGHT AND WRONG.**

RESPONDING TO THE CHALLENGE

What are we to make of this challenge? How should we respond to it? There are at least three responses we ought to make to it.

1. Understand the challenge. Define *impose*. First, we must become clearer on exactly what is meant by this challenge to not *impose*. The word *impose* is notoriously ambiguous, and what is worse, the admonition not to impose gains much of its effect through its ambiguity. We simply can't respond to this challenge until we first understand it. What can it mean to impose our moral values on others?

There are at least two possibilities. First, it may mean forcing other people to *believe* or to adopt our moral viewpoints as their own. That is one possible way to interpret Michael's rebuke to Isaac in the preceding dialogue when he reprimanded him for dogmatically expressing his own moral views as though they were correct and implying that others ought to adopt his moral views as their own. Did Michael mean that Isaac was forcing others to adopt his moral views for themselves?

The problem with this interpretation is that none of us, including Isaac, are able to control the beliefs of others. However strongly we may believe or affirm a particular moral view, we can never force others to believe it for themselves. Even the most dictatorial governments seldom if ever manage to control the thinking of the people under them. The most they can do is force people to *say* they believe certain ideas, but the actual believing of those ideas is up to the people themselves.

Thus it would make no sense for the person uttering the "do not impose" challenge to mean we should stop forcing people to believe or adopt our moral views. This is an instruction to stop doing something that none of us could do in the first place. The admonition not to impose must mean something different.

A second and more likely possible meaning of imposing moral values onto others is forcing them *to live their lives according to our moral values* rather than allowing them the freedom to live by the morals they choose for themselves. This may well be what those issuing the challenge not to impose our values onto others have in mind. On this meaning, they object to the apparent attempt by Isaac to force Michael not to *believe* Isaac's moral values but rather to *live* according to Isaac's moral values, whether Michael believes those values or not. An external forcing of a lifestyle onto people is what is objectionable.

But there is confusion here too. The reality is that from time to time in a free and democratic society we all are compelled to live according to some values and rules we don't appreciate and would not choose for ourselves. We live with speed limits, tax laws, laws against drinking and driving, vandalism, stealing, child abuse and a host of other activities some people would like to do. It is the job of government to establish laws for the good of society, which it then imposes on its citizens and enforces with the appropriate agencies. This kind of imposition is unavoidable in any properly functioning society. Furthermore, virtually every law reflects someone's ideas of right and wrong.

The question is whether these actions by government constitute an imposition of other people's values onto us in any wrong or pernicious sense? It hardly seems so, since the alternative would mean abandoning governmental rule, leaving us in a state described by Thomas Hobbes as "solitary, poor, nasty, brutish, and short."[1]

But perhaps those issuing the challenge to not impose don't have governments in mind but those *individuals* who try to force others to live by their own moral values. If this is what is intended, however, we must ask a second question: To what degree *could* any of us, as individuals in free and democratic societies, force others to live according to our moral values even if we wanted to?

This is a critically important question because the reality is that in such societies, even if we wanted to, few of us as individuals have the power to force others to live the way we think they should. The most any of us can do is express and advocate our moral views and try to convince others to adopt them for themselves. We might even go so far as to try to lobby our governments to have our moral values reflected in public policy. A number of means for this are open to any citizen.

So the key question we must ask is whether it constitutes an imposition of our moral values onto others to express our moral views, to get involved in the democratic process, to lobby, to campaign and to advocate certain policies and laws that we believe to be good for our societies. Do these actions constitute imposing our moral values on others?

It is exceedingly difficult to see this kind of activity as an imposition of values on others in any inappropriate sense. In fact, isn't this precisely what any properly functioning democracy invites its citizens to do? And when people do *not* get involved in this process and then later complain about a particular policy, don't we retort that they have no right to complain since they didn't get involved in the process when they could have? For us to go to these same people and tell them they have no right to get involved because that would be imposing their moral values onto others is simply hypocritical.

---

[1]Thomas Hobbes, *Leviathan* (Indianapolis: Liberal Arts Press, 1983), p. 107.

Clearly the word *impose* is the wrong word to describe this type of activity, and we would be wise to point this out to those issuing the challenge to not impose our values on others. None of us can truly impose our moral values onto others even if we want to. The vast majority of us in democratic societies are simply not in a position to impose *anything* on *anyone*. The most we can do is try to influence public policy through democratic processes, which are open to all citizens, and then hope for the best when the legislators cast their votes.

2. Call for consistency. A second response to this challenge not to impose our moral values onto others is to call people who issue this challenge to be consistent. It's true that a person with a religious worldview speaks from a particular perspective or worldview and he or she should admit it, but so does the person issuing the challenge not to impose one's morality onto others. The reality is that we all have a way of seeing and understanding the world whether it be religious, naturalist, humanist or secularist. None of us live in a vacuum or speak from one. We all live and think within a framework of ideas that provides the very assumptions of our thought, the things we simply take for granted.

This framework of our thought determines the way we ask questions about the world, and it has a profound effect on our instinctive reactions to it. Most important for our discussion, it also shapes the moral values we hold since they flow from it. What this means is that we all hold moral values, flowing from our worldview, that aren't embraced by everyone else. This fact is as true for the people uttering the challenge not to impose as it is for everyone else. In fact, this very challenge is itself a moral statement, which flows from a particular worldview. We must graciously, yet resolutely, call those who issue this challenge to consistency.

The upshot is that for us to tell people that they should not express or advocate their values because not everyone holds to their worldview is simply foolish. On that principle no one could ever advocate anything, including the person advocating the principle that we shouldn't impose our morality on others.

3. Don't allow your moral view to be easily "written off" as religious. We should make it difficult for people to label our moral positions "religious viewpoints" and thereby write them off as irrelevant to people who may not share our religious views. This is a common way of marginalizing entire moral positions, and it's important to see how this works.

Suppose a religious person who stands against the production of human embryos for the purpose of research was pointedly asked *why* she took this moral position. How might she answer? She may respond that she believes this practice is wrong because it involves murdering the tiniest human beings, and the sixth commandment says "Thou shall not murder."[2]

If she were to answer this way, she would probably be told very quickly that this shows beyond doubt that her view is distinctly religious, and as such it should not be imposed on others who don't hold her religious perspectives. And this is how the objection works. Her *reason* for holding her moral view appears to be obviously religious. Therefore her *viewpoint* itself is a religious one that must not be imposed on others. But is it?

This is an important question because much depends on it for understanding the challenge to not impose our moral values onto others. Perhaps the person assuming that the woman's view is religious has moved too quickly. The fact is that so-called religious reasons could be given for many current moral viewpoints on most moral questions, and we must ask whether this fact instantly turns all of these viewpoints into religious views that can't be imposed on people who don't share those religious perspectives?

Something has gone wrong with this reasoning. Obviously, the fact that religious-oriented reasons *can* be given in favor of specific moral positions does not automatically turn those viewpoints into "religious views" that can then be written off or ignored. If it did, we couldn't advocate laws regarding almost any practice, including murder, income-tax evasion, stealing, fraud and so on.

---

[2]For a fuller statement on positions very similar to this, see Focus on the Family's statement on human embryo stem-cell research at <www.family.org/cforum/fosi/bioethics/facts/a0027738.cfm>. See also a letter distributed to United States senators by the United States Conference of Catholic Bishops on March 3, 2000, at <www.usccb.org/prolife/issues/bioethic/keeler0300.htm> in which Cardinal William H. Keeler said embryonic stem-cell research "kills the unborn child."

Perhaps we should ask how this person's viewpoint on human embryos is more religious than, for example, the view that stealing, cheating, murder, rape or slavery are wrong. Religious-sounding reasons could be given against these actions as well, and in fact many people with religious convictions would indeed have religious-oriented reasons as their most fundamental grounds for objecting to these practices as well. Of course, nonreligious-oriented reasons could also be given against these actions.

> **GOD HAS GOOD REASONS FOR EVERY MORAL TEACHING HE HAS SET OUT.**

The kernel of truth we must not overlook here is that for most moral positions both religious- and nonreligious-oriented reasons are available. Indeed, it would be an interesting challenge to try to find a viewpoint on any moral or legal issue for which someone could not or has not come up with both kinds of reasons in support.

People giving religious-oriented reasons for their moral position usually believe that what is really wrong with certain practices is that they violate the will of God. They would also do well to remember that if God decreed certain actions to be either good or not, then he must have had reasons for doing so. Perhaps God knows that a certain act or practice will enhance one's health, well-being, relationships or personal peace of mind and that acting in the opposite way will tend to be destructive in all these areas.

Indeed, C. S. Lewis has argued convincingly that God has good reasons for every moral teaching he has set out. Lewis terms God's moral teachings his "rules for the running of the human machine" and asserts that human beings everywhere ignore these moral rules at their own peril because "every moral rule is there to prevent a breakdown, or a strain, or a friction, in the running of that machine."[3]

---

[3]C. S. Lewis, *Mere Christianity* (New York: Macmillan, 1952), p. 69.

The point is: there may be many good reasons standing behind our moral positions that are not overtly religious-sounding, and we should search these out and present them as effectively as we can. It is one way of demonstrating the wisdom or benefit of our moral positions for people in general. Doing so can also blunt the challenge that our moral positions are religious because we hold them for religious reasons.

What steps can we take to make it more difficult for people to label a moral position religious, thereby giving themselves permission to write it off? In the debate series I was involved in, it became clear in the first debate that this approach was going to be a key part of my opponent's argument, that since I spoke from an overall religious perspective, my view on the question was obviously a religious view that I had no right to impose on others who weren't religious. It was an attempt to marginalize my entire position.

As the debate series progressed, I developed my response to this line of reasoning and made the following four points. I believe they could be part of any strategy for making it difficult for people to write off anyone's viewpoint as religious.

First, I asserted the simple fact that even though religious-sounding reasons *can* be given in favor of specific viewpoints, this does not automatically make them "religious viewpoints" that can then be written off or ignored. If it did, we couldn't advocate laws regarding almost any practice, including murder, income-tax evasion, stealing or fraud, because religious-sounding reasons could be given against all of these as well.

Second, I pointed out that in my opening remarks I had presented no overtly religious arguments for my position. I had presented a number of other arguments that my opponent now needed to respond to. Simply pointing out my overall worldview perspective was not a proper response to the arguments I had presented.

My third response in the debate was to point out that this approach seemed to betray a deep-seated, inherent religious bigotry. It implied that whereas nonreligious worldviews or moral positions are perfectly legitimate for discussion in the public square, religious ones are not, simply because they are religious. This shows a discriminatory attitude that should have no place in open debate in a free and pluralistic society.

Fourth, I pointed out that in reality the issue we were debating was not a religious versus nonreligious issue. There are both kinds of people in both camps on this issue. Retired Episcopalian bishop John Shelby Spong of Newark, New Jersey, is a well-known example of a prominent religious figure who takes the opposite position to mine.[4] And this is the case with many moral questions in our culture. It is usually far from the mark to label one view *the religious view* and thereby imply that all religious people will be of one mind on it.

How might Isaac reply to Michael based on these four responses? Michael has just accused Isaac of imposing his moral values on others by "spouting off" his personal moral views on a variety of issues from animal rights to abortion to euthanasia, implying that his views are right and that if other people don't agree with them, they are wrong. His particular concern is that Isaac will try to push his moral views onto others who don't agree with them. Imagine the conversation continued this way:

Isaac: You're right, I did express my views on a few moral issues with those people. I'm even considering writing the newspaper with some of my convictions on stem-cell research and abortion.

Michael: Not again!

Isaac: Yes. I have much more to say about them now, so this time I think I'll send copies to a couple of local legislators too.

Michael: So you *are* going to try to push your values onto the rest of us. At least you're honest about it. But what gives you that right?

Isaac: Don't *you* express your views on moral issues? Don't *you* try to influence public policy in a way you believe to be good?

---

[4]In a series of debates I participated in with Dr. Faye Girsh, international director of the Hemlock Society, in October 1997, she repeatedly asserted that John Shelby Spong, retired bishop of Newark, New Jersey, shared her view that physician-assisted suicide should be legalized.

Michael: Yes, but I'm not religious. You are, and you're trying to impose your religious morals on the rest of us who are not religious.

Isaac: Does everyone agree with *your* moral values?

Michael: No, I guess not.

Isaac: That's a timid answer to an obvious question, and an important one too.

Michael: Alright, I admit it, not everyone agrees with my moral values.

Isaac: So we both have values not shared by everyone. And when *you* argue that certain laws should be enacted into public policy, aren't you doing the same thing you were just saying I was doing, imposing your moral values on others who do not necessarily agree with you?

Michael: I don't like the word *impose*.

Isaac: Neither do I, but since you raised it, could we talk about it for a moment? I've got some questions about that word.

Michael: Be my guest.

Isaac: Is it imposing one's moral values onto others to get involved in the democratic process, to lobby and campaign, and to try to influence public policy in a way that you believe is good?

Michael: Well if you put it that way . . .

Isaac: Doesn't democracy even invite us to do this? Is that really imposing one's morals onto others? How could it be?

Michael: No, I suppose it's not.

Isaac: I agree, because if it is, then everyone who tries to influence public policy this way would be guilty of imposing his or her moral values on the rest of us. Let's face it. We both know that the word *impose* is the wrong word to describe what we or anyone else are doing when we do this.

Michael: OK, let me grant you this: as long as this is what we are doing, we are not imposing our moral values onto others.

Isaac: That was easy. I'm glad we cleared that up.

Michael: Whoa, not so fast. I still disagree with what you're doing.

Isaac (somewhat taken aback): But I thought you just agreed that . . .

Michael: Hey, I agreed that it's possible to get involved in the democratic process without necessarily imposing one's own moral values onto others. And that's all I agreed to, because there's a serious difference between what *you* are doing and what *I* am doing. I heard you back there talking to those people.

Isaac: How's that again? What difference?

Michael: You are *restricting* people from doing something they want to do. I'm not. If people want an abortion or euthanasia, I say go ahead. If they choose not to do these things, they don't have to. But *you* are trying to enact laws to stop people from doing these things because you think they are wrong. That is imposing.

Isaac: And you don't do this?

Michael: No way! Not a chance!

Isaac: How do you feel about child pornography?

Michael: Child pornography. It's disgusting! It harms children. Perhaps you've heard I'm president of the local chapter of CCPC, Citizens Concerned for the Protection of Children. That's why I got involved. I saw too many children taken advantage of for child pornography. We've recently established a website that identifies legislators who have voted against anti-child-pornography legislation. As far as I'm concerned, those people are scum. Children need the legal protection. They're in a position to provide it, but they're not doing it.

Isaac: Should child pornography be illegal?

Michael: Of course it should be illegal!

Isaac: What about rape, murder, speeding, tax evasion or driving on any side of the road you please?

Michael: Yeah, what about these things?

Isaac: Should they be illegal too?

Michael (looking irritated): Obviously. Stupid question.

Isaac: Even though some people *want* to do those things?

Michael: Yes, and your point is?

Isaac: That you do it too.

Michael: I do *what* too?

Isaac: You impose your values onto others who don't agree with you or don't want to live by your values. Every legal restriction is a restriction on someone's choice, and you just said you're in favor of legal restrictions on all those activities I just mentioned.

Michael: Sure, I'm in favor of laws to prevent someone from harming another person. Child pornography harms children. Driving on any side of the road would cause people to die. We need laws against these actions to protect people.

Isaac: Let me get this straight. You believe it is legitimate to argue for laws you believe are necessary to protect people even though some others may disagree with you?

Michael: Yes, and that's the only reason.

Isaac: Exactly.

Michael: What?

Isaac: I said exactly because that is why I think abortion should be restricted by law.

Michael (rolling his eyes): Boy you pro-lifers are something. Sometimes I think your collars are too tight, and you're cutting off oxygen to the brain. Abortion is different. Who is being harmed in an abortion?

Isaac: The unborn, whom I believe to be fully human persons in embryonic form, and therefore deserving of protection like all other human beings.

Michael: The fetus—fully human—with the same rights as other humans? I don't believe that for a minute.

Isaac: Yes, I know. You and I disagree about who or what is being harmed in an abortion. Since I believe the fetus is human, a tiny person in embryonic form, I believe an abortion harms, in fact kills, a person, and didn't you just say it is legitimate to argue for a law you believe is necessary to protect people even though others may disagree with you?

Michael: Yes, I said that but . . .

Isaac: So you don't really have a problem with what I'm doing, do you? You just called it legitimate.

Michael (pausing): But aren't you forgetting something?

Isaac: Probably. What?

Michael: Those abortion protesters. Surely, you admit if anyone is imposing their morality onto others, *they* are. They're out there actively trying to stop people from having abortions.

Isaac: Yes, they're just as bad as those logging protesters and those seal-hunt protesters, not to mention Martin Luther King Jr. and his civil rights protests. Do you condemn those too? After all, they've engaged in civil disobedience too, and they've tried to stop people from doing something they want to do.

Michael: I didn't used to condemn them, but I've changed my mind and I do now.

Isaac: That was a good change of mind, at least if you're going to condemn abortion protesters. Because if you condemn one but not the others, you'd be glaringly inconsistent since they're all out there doing the same thing, trying to prevent people from engaging in some activity they want to engage in.

Michael: Which is why I disagree with them all.

Isaac: So what you're really disagreeing with is civil disobedience in all its forms, not just abortion protesters. And you may be right. That's a debatable point, but let's not be too quick here.

Michael: Why not?

Isaac: Think about it. Are they really so different from the rest of us who lobby for new laws to restrict certain activities? In both cases we're trying to stop people from doing things they want to do. In civil disobedience the people themselves try to stop the activities. In the other, we get the government and police to stop them for us.

Michael: But this is different.

Isaac: How?

Michael: These people are breaking the law.

Isaac: True. That is the difference. In one case, we use legal means to stop people from doing something they want to do. In the other case, they have given up on those and have turned to other means.

Michael: Which are illegal.

Isaac: Yes, you keep saying that. That's why they call it civil *disobedience*. I think that although this should be a last resort, history has shown that governments are sometimes like big ships, slow to change course to bring about justice.

Michael: So you're saying people can just take the law into their own hands. That sounds like vigilante justice.

Isaac: Actually, if you practice it properly, civil disobedience is the furthest thing from vigilante justice.[5] What I'm saying is that sometimes individual people recognize the injustice of a particular law or public policy and are willing to put themselves at risk to force the issue, to appeal to people's sense of justice and end an unjust practice.

Michael: Such as?

Isaac: I'm thinking of slavery and the underground railroad, Martin Luther King Jr. and the civil rights protests he led, the ten Boom family, Gandhi, the Hebrew midwives in Exodus, and the followers of Jesus in the New Testament.

Michael (under his breath): I'm not sure if I want to admit it, but there may be more to imposing one's morality onto others than it first appears.

---

[5]Political philosopher John Rawls sets out conditions under which he believes civil disobedience may be engaged in, in his article titled, "The Justification of Civil Disobedience," in *Readings in Social and Political Philosophy,* ed. Robert M. Stewart (Oxford: Oxford University Press, 1986), esp. pp. 80-82. For another helpful discussion of civil disobedience see Richard A. Wasserstrom, "The Obligation to Obey the Law," *UCLA Law Review* 10 (1963): 78-87.

7

WHERE HAVE WE COME SO FAR?

Marking Our Foundations

In chapter one we described this book as a map or guidebook to help us engage others on moral issues that sometimes confuse us and occasionally drive us around the bend. This map has taken us through new ways of thinking about morality, confusing moral messages and complex dilemmas resulting from our exploding technology. These have all combined to radically change the moral landscape and to raise a host of questions that make the task of engaging others on important moral issues neither simple nor clear. Is there any such thing as real, objective good and evil in the first place, or is morality strictly a private and personal matter? Is morality purely subjective and relative? Is it really wrong to impose our moral values on others? Is it especially wrong to do so if our moral position happens to be viewed as a religious one? And ought we to view tolerance as the supreme cultural virtue in our pluralistic society? If so, does this mean we are to accept all moral points of view as roughly equal and stop claiming we have moral truth?

FOUNDATIONAL MORAL TRUTHS THAT MATTER

As we have worked our way through these questions and others like them, we have been forced to recognize a number of foundational moral truths. We have bumped up against some of the moral foundations, rock-solid ideas, that have guided us through confusing issues and perspectives. It is now time for us to state these truths explicitly, to bring them out into the open for all to see. This will enable us to understand them clearly and get a firm grip on them, something we will need if we hope to engage others skillfully in discussion of moral issues.

Once we do this it will be time for us to ask that all-important question: how can we, as individual people, make a difference in our culture? Is it even possible to have an influence on the social and moral questions that virtually all of society recognizes are important? That question will be the focus of our final chapter.

Since we have already seen and dealt with these foundational truths, we need not explain them at great length here, only make them explicit. Until now, they have been operating in the background. What then are these foundational moral truths?

There is objective moral truth, and deep down we all know it. This means that, purely, morality is not subjective and relative, an idea that could be stated as a separate foundational moral truth but, in reality, is the flip side of this one. We recognize actions and attitudes that are either commendable or ought to be condemned, whether in ourselves or in other people. Furthermore, we expect others to recognize them too, and they do. Put simply, objective moral truth is extraordinarily difficult to deny, and virtually no one manages to do so successfully. This provides the basis for the second foundational truth.

Morality is not strictly a private, personal matter. Indeed this truth flows directly from the previous one. If there were no such thing as objective moral truth, if morality were purely subjective and relative, then morality would indeed be a private matter and nothing more. But it isn't, and attempting to maintain that it is will lead us headlong into confusion and contradiction, just as it did for Michael in an early dialogue with Isaac. Michael believed morality really was a purely private matter, and this led him to tell Isaac in no uncertain terms that he ought to respect and be tolerant toward other people's moral views. He should recognize that they are just as "right" for them as Isaac's are for him.

But notice what has happened here. We suddenly have a moral directive, namely, that we ought to be respectful and tolerant of other people's moral views. But if morality really is purely private and personal, then the person giving us this directive should have kept his moral views to him- or herself. What business does anyone have dictating his or her moral views to anyone else? The upshot is that being told to live as though your morals are strictly private and personal is being told to live in a way that is, at the very least, incoherent and, at worst, impossible. How then should we live out the truths that objective moral value exists and morality is not merely private? Important clarifications are needed, and this leads us to the next three foundational moral truths.

Getting involved in the democratic process and advocating specific public policies and laws we believe to be good for our society does not necessarily constitute an imposition of our values on others in any improper way. In fact, this is precisely what every properly functioning democracy invites its citizens to do, and it's hypocritical to tell people who get involved in this way that they have no right to do this because they would be imposing their values onto others. Clearly the word *impose* is the wrong word to describe this type of activity.

In reality, very few of us could truly impose our moral values onto others even if we wanted to. The vast majority of us are not in a position to impose anything on anyone. The most we can do is try to influence public policy through democratic processes that are open to all citizens for this very purpose.

Tolerance is compatible with truth and is a wonderful virtue in a pluralistic society—when it is carefully understood. Tolerance does not require agreement or affirmation or endorsement, as many in our culture tend to assume. In fact, it makes no sense to speak of tolerating things I already agree with. If I agree with something, I do not need to tolerate it. Tolerance is an attitude that says, "I accept your right to say or do something I disagree with." As such, it actually presupposes *disagreement* with what I am tolerating.

This also means tolerance is compatible with truth. Without different points of view (that is, disagreement about what is true or good), the need for tolerance doesn't arise. It is perfectly possible to hold a viewpoint I believe is true and at the same time be tolerant toward other views I think are false.

The relevance of this for anyone wishing to engage others in moral discourse is obvious. Any person living in a pluralistic society will soon encounter others who don't share his or her convictions about what is true or good. These moments are opportunities to show tolerance.

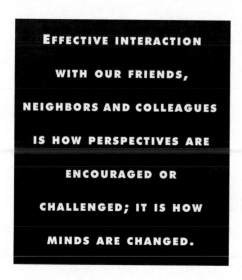

EFFECTIVE INTERACTION WITH OUR FRIENDS, NEIGHBORS AND COLLEAGUES IS HOW PERSPECTIVES ARE ENCOURAGED OR CHALLENGED; IT IS HOW MINDS ARE CHANGED.

The only question remaining is when to show tolerance and when not to, and it's clear that there are times when an intolerant attitude is called for. We rightly proclaim zero tolerance against societal ills such as drinking and driving, child abuse and attacks on women. We have learned that this is the way to protect what we deeply value in society. Children are safer in a world where there is no tolerance for abuse of them. We are all more protected in societies that have no tolerance for attacks on us.

The fact that religious-sounding reasons can be given for a specific moral position does not automatically make that position a "religious position" that can then be written off or ignored as irrelevant for others who do not share that religious perspective. If it did, we couldn't advocate laws regarding almost any practice, since religious-sounding reasons can be and often are given for virtually any moral position.

The last three foundational moral truths relate to the cultural situation we find early in this new millennium. Indeed they are indispensable if we are to successfully engage the pervasive moral ideas in our culture.

There are few if any true moral relativists. Our actions betray our true convictions. While many in our culture *say* morality is subjective and relative, virtually all *act* as though it is objectively real. Few of us manage to escape the notion that certain things are truly good while others are genuinely evil. It looks as though we are going to have to decide: will we be moral relativists, as so many claim to be, or will we carry on commending and condemning various activities, attitudes and characteristics, as we so readily do? Doing both leads to a fundamental confusion.

Moral confusion cannot go on forever, whether in the mind of a single person or within society as a whole. A moral perspective that includes conflicting ideas or principles simply can't be lived out. Given the right circumstances, a person or society will act on one conflicting principle or the other. This has nothing to do with whether we may wish this state of confusion could go on forever or even whether we are concerned about such things as moral confusion. It has to do with the fact that it's impossible to live out conflicting ideas at the same time. It simply can't be done.

In our moral discourse with others, our task is to detect moral confusion, understand it and finally draw it to the attention of those we are in dialogue with. This can provide a wonderful basis for encouraging a person to abandon a moral position he or she can't live out anyway and seek a better one.

No one lives in a vacuum or speaks from one. Everyone speaks from some worldview and set of moral values flowing from it. We have noted that people with religious convictions are sometimes charged with speaking from particular worldviews, and since others do not share them, they should keep their worldviews and morals to themselves.

The reality is that we all have a way of seeing and understanding the world, whether it be religious, naturalist, humanist, secularist and so forth. This framework of our thought shapes the moral values we hold since they flow from it. The critical point for anyone wishing to engage others in moral discussion is that it is foolish in the extreme for us to tell a person not to express or advocate certain values because not everyone holds to the same worldview. On that principle, no one could advocate anything.

These are some of the foundations, and we have seen them rise to the fore in the preceding chapters, both in the dialogues and the following explanations. They have guided us as we have wrestled with some of the confusing pitfalls and challenges we will experience if we choose to engage others in discussion of moral issues in the twenty-first century. And they have brought us to the most important question of all, which is: how we can make a difference in this culture when it comes to the important moral issues of the day? No doubt, our primary tool for making such a difference is effective dialogue. Effective interaction with our friends, neighbors and colleagues is how perspectives are encouraged or challenged; it is how minds are changed. When minds change, culture itself changes. And so the critical question becomes: Can these foundational truths guide us and make our interaction with others more effective? It is to this final question that we now turn.

8

CAN I MAKE
A DIFFERENCE?

The Battle for Change

It is fair to assume that you wouldn't have read this far unless you felt a passion for your culture. You've seen the injustices and moral lapses, and you can't turn a blind eye to them. You want to do something about what you see. You want to make your society better, healthier, more decent, humane, just, more respectful of human dignity and of all kinds of life. And this is the new challenge before us: how can you, or any of us, make this kind of difference in our society? Is it even realistic to think we could make such a difference?

Simply put, the question is this: Are we dreaming to think that individual people can engage fellow citizens on the social and moral issues we feel passionate about and actually cause a difference in the way our society thinks or acts about them? Are we deluding ourselves to think we could affect the tide in this way? Are the issues too big and unwieldy, the systems of power, law and public opinion too vast and too established for our puny efforts to have any serious affect on them?

Before getting discouraged about the daunting nature of this task, let's not forget that societies do change one way or the other over time. They don't remain stagnant in their social and moral habits and trends any more than they do in their fashion or culinary habits. Western culture is not the same as it was 30, 50 or 150 years ago. What was morally acceptable or commendable then is not necessarily so now. We only have to think of changing Western attitudes toward such things as the environment, human rights (specifically the rights of women and minorities), abortion, sexuality and marriage to see that attitudes and moral perspectives don't remain the same.

And when moral and social change has occurred in any society, it has often been as the result of one or a few individuals working hard to bring about such change. The point is that individual people can and have made a difference. Certain names stand out whose legacies are profound in this way: General William Booth, Mohandas Gandhi, Corrie ten Boom, Abraham Lincoln, Martin Luther King Jr. and William Wilberforce, to name a few. These were people who left the world a different place than they found it. Indeed, the national consciousness of many countries has been deeply affected by their actions.

What did they and others like them do that was so profound? The answer, in a nutshell, is that they saw injustice, often a particular kind of injustice, and gave their lives to the task of ending it, usually at great personal cost. The result, invariably, was that the people of their day were better off because of what these heroes did. General William Booth saw poor people receive food and a place to sleep and build new lives for themselves. Corrie ten Boom saw Jewish people, who otherwise would have been slaughtered or subjected to perverse human experiments simply because they were Jews, spared from Nazi atrocities during World War II. William Wilberforce and Abraham Lincoln saw slaves freed. Martin Luther King Jr. saw laws and public policies changed so that black people could be treated equally and, in some cases, be given special advantages with the aim of compensating for prior disadvantages. Gandhi saw Indian people begin to receive better treatment at the hands of the British. Many other unsung heroes have made similar differences in their own societies, and the critical question before us now is this: How can we use the principles of the preceding chapters to help make a difference in our culture now?

We have much to learn from the great people of the past about making a difference in our own culture in the twenty-first century. In fact, learning lessons from them is critical if we wish to avoid repeating the mistakes of the past. In almost every case these leaders in moral and social justice spent a lifetime developing skills and methods that can be applied far more broadly than merely to their own cultural issues.

They also developed careful strategies for addressing the particular moral issues of their times, strategies that were guided by the foundational moral truths we have set out in this book at every turn. Not every moral truth we have set out was appealed to for every moral issue they encountered, but that was part of the strategy, learning how and when to appeal to the appropriate foundational moral truth with skill and wisdom.

So it comes down to this. There are *lessons* to be learned in a general way about how others before us have made a difference; there are specific *strategies* to be examined in how they have successfully worked for positive cultural change; and finally there are *foundational moral truths* guiding and undergirding the entire process.

Learning from William Wilberforce

Of the above-mentioned names, one giant stands out: William Wilberforce, a member of the British parliament for forty-five years, who fought to change the heart of his nation. He strove against the entrenched powers and economic structures of his society and was ultimately successful not merely in winning his specific battle—to end slavery in Great Britain—but in kindling the consciences of the people of his society to the need for justice in other areas as well. The far-reaching effects of his efforts are seen in part in the way Western civilization today views slavery. In Wilberforce's day the practice was commonplace. Today it is unthinkable.

Wilberforce lived from 1759 to 1833. His was a privileged background. From his youth he demonstrated considerable personal skills. His humor and wit gained him friends easily, and his intelligence and skill as a debater and orator made him highly successful as a parliamentarian. He was said to have been able to speak to an audience for hours and make people enjoy it.

He also had no use for religion, and consequently fit well into the social scene of London. The city, described as one vast casino, was known for its prestigious private clubs, gambling casinos, brothels and prostitutes who specialized in any manner of perversion desired.

This luxurious lifestyle was underwritten by child labor and the slave trade, which had become not only successful businesses but also national policies. The slave trade was supported by planters and gentlemen who had grown rich through the profits of their trade, and they used these profits to become an increasingly powerful force in parliament. These men would pay up to 5,000 pounds to "buy" boroughs (towns) that sent their representatives to the House of Commons.

> **TRUE CHRISTIANITY NOT ONLY SAVES, IT SERVES.**

Few practices were more entrenched in the economic structure of England than slavery. Challenging it seemed hopeless, although a few religious groups had tried. But the nation had yet to feel the impact of William Wilberforce.

For a time Wilberforce simply enjoyed the social scene and good life available to any young, well-off person of his day. But one day, through the urging of his old schoolmaster, Isaac Milner, Wilberforce agreed to read the Christian Scriptures daily. As his diary from 1785 indicates, this led to a dramatic turning point. Becoming increasingly dissatisfied with his present condition, Wilberforce began referring to himself as "wretched," "blind" and "miserable."

His struggle climaxed when John Newton, a former slave and slave trader who had become a Christian, led Wilberforce to follow Christ. Newton also urged him not to abandon public office but rather to use his position for the good of God's church and the nation. Wilberforce had fundamentally changed, and the nation would soon feel it.

But what did it mean to be a Christian, especially as a member of parliament in the eighteenth century? Wilberforce pondered that question and soon came to the conviction that though his conversion meant that God had eternally rescued his soul, the meaning must go deeper. True Christianity not only saves, it serves, he believed. It must bring God's compassion to the oppressed. It must, in fact, oppose the oppressors.

And here we see Wilberforce's allegiance to the first foundational moral truth set out in chapter seven. There is real objective truth. Some things are genuinely wrong not just for us but for others as well, and the slavery of the British Commonwealth was one of them. Wilberforce knew it, and he became convinced that his countrymen either knew it too or should know it. This unshakable conviction drove virtually everything he did in the battle to end slavery.

Through the influence of a brilliant essayist and clergyman, Thomas Clarkson, whose pamphlets detailed the brutality of the slave trade, Wilberforce's social conscience was kindled. In 1787 he wrote: "Almighty God has set before me two great objectives: the abolition of the slave trade and the reformation of manners [i.e., morals]."[1] With those words, an epic struggle began against the entrenched evils of his day in English society.

Why did he succeed? When we look at his life, there are a number of lessons we can learn that not only accounted for Wilberforce's success but can also contribute to our effectiveness in bringing about moral and social change in our own culture.

MORAL AND SOCIAL JUSTICE: AN INDIVISIBLE WHOLE

The first lesson for us is that Wilberforce saw social justice as an indivisible whole and not as a group of individual practices that could be addressed in isolation from the others. Morality was a matter of the heart. If a person had grown cold toward social justice, that coldness would work itself out consistently in one's willingness to tolerate a whole range of unjust practices. Wilberforce understood that the same hearts that allowed human slavery would eventually tolerate other injustices as well.

---

[1] Garth Lean, *God's Politician* (Colorado Springs: Helmers & Howard, 1987), p. 47. For a more exhaustive biography of William Wilberforce, see John Pollock's well-known book *Wilberforce* (Belleville, Mich.: Lion, 1986).

This truth was plainly evident in English society. Not only was slavery accepted but child labor was as well. Young children worked up to eighteen hours a day in cotton mills or coal mines for a few shillings a month. Furthermore, while British subjects in India were suffering grim treatment at the hands of Wilberforce's countrymen, harsh debtor laws were keeping many poor English citizens in prisons at home. They were held in prison until they could pay their outstanding debt, but, of course, being in prison allowed them no opportunity to earn money to pay off the debt.

Public executions occurred frequently, often as public sport, with young, petty thieves being executed in the same ceremony as serious criminals, while excited crowds looked on. Meanwhile, on the streets of London hordes of prostitutes (estimated at one-quarter of the women in the city) sold their bodies in increasingly degrading practices. All of these injustices had become part of the established economic and political structure of England, and Wilberforce saw a connection between them all.

He attacked these practices on both personal and institutional levels. During his lifetime Wilberforce regularly gave away one-quarter or more of his income to the poor. He personally paid the bills of many people in prison under the debt laws so they could live productive lives. Along with others, he organized the Society for the Education of Africans, the Society for Bettering the Condition of the Poor and the Society for the Relief of Debtors, which obtained the release of fourteen thousand people from prisons.

MORAL AND SOCIAL JUSTICE: A MATTER OF CAREFUL STRATEGY

A second lesson for us is that the fight for social justice requires a careful strategy. Wilberforce employed one—very little was left to chance. In attacking slavery his strategy included at least three elements that we would do well to emulate.

1. Inform and be informed. Facts. Information. Data. We tend to underestimate the importance of these, but if you have ever attempted to make a case for a cause or viewpoint you believe in, you will know only too well how quickly and resoundingly a shortage of necessary facts can shatter your case. Whether it is details of the practice under consideration, historical data related to it, relevant statistics or knowledge of the other side of the issue, getting the facts usually requires painstaking research and high levels of both tenacity and energy.

Wilberforce worked with facts, many of which were not known to the English public. How many knew, for instance, that slaves were rounded up in Africa, chained, held and then sold to the highest bidder who had come into port? The elderly and unfit were shot or clubbed to death while others, screaming and pleading for mercy, were loaded onto ships, shackled into irons and forced into vile holds where the stench of human waste and vomit was overwhelming.

There the slaves lay on their sides crammed so tightly together that the chest of each was pressed against the sweaty back of the next. Many would die on each trip while others, driven insane, would by killed by the crew. Meanwhile, the crew had the pick of the slave women, making the ship "half bedlam, half brothel," as one captain put it.

As we noted above, his conviction that objective moral value existed and that the slave trade was genuinely wrong drove Wilberforce's strategy. It was now coupled with the corresponding flip-side moral truth that morality is not all subjective and relative. It couldn't be if objective moral value existed, and in this case Wilberforce was facing a practice that wasn't simply immoral relative to certain contexts or situations; it was wrong and vile for all people in every place it was practiced. So he attacked it everywhere he found it.

It was facts that had kindled his social conscience to recognize a wrong he had overlooked before, and he was convinced they could do the same for his fellow citizens. If they didn't recognize the evil of this practice already, many would if they too were simply made aware of precisely what it involved. The reality was that without huge numbers of his fellow citizens coming to recognize the genuine evil of the slave trade, it would never be ended, and the horrible plight of the slaves would continue.

Getting the facts required great effort and expense in research and travel, but he knew that without them he had nothing to oppose the powerful economic and political establishment that had come to depend on this trade for its prosperity and power.

Through pamphlets and speeches in the House of Commons and elsewhere, Wilberforce made these facts known to an often shocked public. Armed with them, he called slavery a "national crime" and "a course of wickedness and cruelty as never before disgraced a Christian country."[2]

Anyone could say these words, even with great dramatic flair, but only someone with the facts to support them could say them with credibility and thereby grab the sustained attention of the public. These facts, once made known to the public, spoke for themselves. They made it impossible for Wilberforce's opponents to ignore his severe descriptions of slavery or treat such descriptions with disdain.

Here we see Wilberforce being driven by another foundational moral truth, one which is difficult for some in our culture to accept, namely, that morality is not a strictly personal and private matter. Slavery was one practice he believed to be genuinely wrong, and the fact that others around him held moral views that regarded it as acceptable conduct did not change this fact. It didn't make the practice of slavery somehow "right for them." Different moral views are not all equally correct, and in this case those who regarded slavery as morally permissible were told their moral position was simply wrong. The onus was then on them to demonstrate that a practice as cruel as the one Wilberforce had laid out in grisly detail was somehow morally acceptable. Wilberforce neither shrank from denouncing this practice nor from calling for its end.

In all of this Wilberforce was operating in accord with yet another foundational moral truth, namely, that advocating a public policy we believe to be good for our society, however vigorously, does not necessarily constitute an imposition of our moral values on others in an improper way. As a parliamentarian he, more than most, recognized that every law is a restriction on someone's choice, and yet no nation can function with-

---

[2]Pollock, *Wilberforce*, p. 143.

out them. The only question is which laws will be enacted.

Wilberforce also knew full well that entire industries would be adversely affected if the slave trade ever ended and that people in them would feel that disagreeable laws had been imposed on them. None of this, however, stood in the way of Wilberforce using the democratic processes available to him to advocate public policies that would help the slaves, children, prisoners and others.

2. Have answers for opponents. We've all seen people confidently express their own views on issues and voice disdain for opposing positions. Perhaps we have done it ourselves. I have occasionally asked students and others who I've heard doing this whether they are able to explain a viewpoint they disagree with to me in a way that would satisfy someone who believes it. My question is usually met with a blank stare that becomes even blanker when I follow up that question by asking if they are able to articulate two or three of the strongest arguments *for* the view they are scorning.

Understanding opposing views and what can be said in favor of them is not something we come by naturally. We usually have to be pushed into it. But forcing ourselves to do this is indispensable if we hope to effectively engage others and bring about real positive change in our culture.

There are at least three reasons why this is critical if we wish to make an impact: First, virtually any position can be presented persuasively if it is allowed to stand alone, uncontested. This is especially true if the ideas are articulated by a skilled orator. The Bill Clintons and Ronald Reagans of this world have been able to make virtually any view sound convincing. (Of course, having a team of talented speech writers doesn't hurt either.) The real question, however, is whether the case is still compelling when laid side by side with an opposing case or an alternative position that is also skillfully articulated. Unless we are able to show that it is, we have no right to expect others to be convinced by what we have to say. In fact, they may be wiser to stick with their own point of view for the time being.

Second, honesty compels us to examine the opposing case to see how it stacks up against our own. How can we in good conscience continue to believe our own viewpoint is superior, or act on it, if we have not examined the opposing case and found it wanting? After all, it ought to be the truth we are genuinely seeking in these matters, and so long as we have not examined the other side of the issue, the possibility remains that it is the better viewpoint, the one we should and would adopt if only we took a good look at it.

Third, if we want to adequately respond to opposing positions, which we must if we hope to bring about real change in people's thinking, we must first understand them. There simply is no shortcut here. Responding to positions we have not examined or understood leads to straw man arguments where we distort our opponents' positions, making them appear to be weak or silly, and then easily shoot them down. That is not only dishonest; it's also ineffective since it leaves the original, actual position untouched. It also discredits our own position by implying that the only way it can appear stronger than an opposing viewpoint is by distorting that other viewpoint.

Wilberforce familiarized himself with his opponents' arguments against his claims and developed thoughtful and compelling responses to them, responses guided by other specific foundational moral truths. His opponents argued that slaves were not truly human but were, in the words of one court decision, simply chattels. The same decision had established that a ship's captain had the right at law to dump as many overboard as he wished "without any suggestion of cruelty or surmise of impropriety."[3] This had become common opinion concerning the moral status of the slaves. Humanness had been, in effect, redefined in such a way that the slaves were not included in its definition, and the consequences were breathtaking. If slaves weren't human, there was no moral duty to treat them as though they were. This common assumption allowed the opinion-makers of the day—and indeed the general English public—to treat slaves in a grisly manner and at the same time claim to have a high regard for humanity.

Further, his opponents argued that Wilberforce's view that slaves were

---

[3]Lean, *God's Politician*, pp. 49-51.

human was merely his own personal religious view and should not be imposed on others as public policy. "Humanity," argued the Earl of Abingdon on one occasion, "is a private feeling, not a public principle to act upon."[4]

Supporters of the slave trade also argued that the economy would suffer a fundamental upset if this institution were abolished. Abolition would instantly annihilate a trade that annually employed upward of 5,500 sailors and 160 ships, and whose exports amounted to 800,000 pounds.

Wilberforce and others responded by continually returning to the question of the humanity of the slaves. They pointed out the confused moral perspectives of the slave traders, in keeping with another foundational moral truth. This provided a basis for urging these traders to abandon their moral positions. Wilberforce did this by reminding his opponents that, try as they might, they could not escape the reality that the slaves really were human, and they knew it. Didn't supporters of the slave trade have sex with slaves? Didn't supporters allow their children to play with the children of the slaves? Didn't supporters treat the slave trader with contempt due to the despicable nature of his work? Such behavior on the part of Wilberforce's opponents made no sense, he argued, if slaves were not human. In fact, it was utterly confusing with tragic results.

But if slaves were truly human after all, then slavery was not merely a religious matter, argued Wilberforce, appealing to yet another foundational moral truth. He refused to allow his moral position to be written off as merely his own religious perspective. People did not need to be religious to know that humans ought not be treated in the way the slaves were. Furthermore, it made little difference to the argument that dire economic consequences could result from ending slavery. If the slaves really were human, then slavery was immoral and foul regardless of the economic consequences. And the responses went on and on, each preceded by a careful understanding of his opponents' arguments.

3. Point fingers backward, not just forward. People who have tried to argue someone out of a viewpoint have undoubtedly experienced the

---

[4]Ibid.

surprise of having the person whose mind they were seeking to change
become defensive and actually begin to stick up for his or her viewpoint
even more passionately than before. Indeed, as a professor of university
students, I have seen this phenomenon occur in my classes over the
years, often in uncanny ways. As a means of encouraging students to engage with specific ethical issues, I occasionally assign them, either indi-
vidually or as small groups, the task of defending a particular viewpoint
on a specific issue in class debate settings. The assigned viewpoints are
randomly chosen, without regard for the students' real views on the matter. In no time, after enduring the attacks of opposing groups, students
often move far beyond the class requirement of bringing to light strong
points in favor of the assigned viewpoint and begin to defend this view
with increasing gusto, sometimes actually adopting it as their own personal stance before the class is over. It's not unusual for students to exit
class after these in-house debates with a zeal for their newfound personal
views matched only by the fervor seen at a rock concert or the World Series, all because "their view" was assailed by their fellow students.

At times I find it humorous. At other times it is downright unnerving
as I realize the power of this technique for "messing with students'
minds," as the students themselves have good-naturedly put it to me.

The reality is that none of us are very good at separating our viewpoints from our own identities. When our *views* are attacked, and especially if the attack includes scorn, *we* often feel attacked or scorned.
When that happens, we react defensively, which usually means we leap
to the defense of the viewpoint that was being attacked and ridiculed.

This, of course, is partly because the same inability to separate a *viewpoint* from the *person* is found in the one making the argument as well.
All too often, whether intentionally or otherwise, we attack the person
holding the viewpoint rather than limiting our remarks to the viewpoint
itself. It is an easy mistake to make since, after all, what kind of people
would carry out shameful practices or hold foolish viewpoints? Shameful or foolish people, of course. At least that is what is implied unless the
one making the argument takes great pains to avoid this implication.

What this means is that any time we argue against someone's viewpoint, we run the risk of pushing that person further into the grasp of the very position we were trying to discourage. This can be discouraging, and in fact, this phenomenon has caused some to wonder whether we should abandon the whole process of debate and argument altogether. Isn't the whole approach simply antagonistic and counterproductive? If so, then why keep on with it?[5]

Wilberforce did not share this pessimistic view of debate, but he did appear to understand this reality about argumentation very well. He knew that if his arguments against slavery, child labor or debtor laws, or any other shameful practice turned into accusations or attacks on the people who advocated these practices, or even if they were perceived as such, they would tend to have the opposite effect of what he was hoping for. Rather than moving people *from* these practices, they would likely make them even fiercer defenders of them.

How did Wilberforce deal with this reality? Not by giving up on debate altogether. For a parliamentarian such as Wilberforce, that option was unthinkable. Rather, he demonstrated unusual wisdom in choosing an approach we can learn from. With a stroke of genius—and humility—he went beyond simply avoiding personal attacks and actually took great care to include himself in the guilt whenever he attacked any shameful practice. He referred to slavery as "a course of wickedness and cruelty as never before disgraced a Christian country." "I mean not to accuse anyone," he said, "but to take the shame upon myself, in common indeed with the whole Parliament of Britain, for having suffered this horrid trade to be carried on under their authority. We are all guilty—we ought all to plead guilty, and not to exculpate ourselves by throwing the blame on others."[6] Rather than setting himself up as the innocent party

---

[5]Over the years I have encountered people who question the value of argument and debate on this ground. At least one person has gone further and suggested to a colleague of mine that it might be wise for those who debate important theological and ethical issues with others to actually lose the occasional debate. If this suggestion were to be taken seriously, it could, I assume, be done only by either purposely leaving out arguments in favor of one's own position or intentionally misrepresenting and weakening the position sufficiently so that the opposing viewpoint would appear stronger. In either case, the entire process would become a deceptive sham. It seems wiser to follow Wilberforce's approach outlined in this chapter.

[6]Lean, *God's Politician*, p. 53.

attacking the guilty, he positioned himself also as a member of the society that was practicing and benefiting from these shameful practices. His call was for others to join him in removing this burden of guilt from the nation he loved.

The genius of this approach is that it made it virtually impossible for anyone to feel personally attacked when Wilberforce called on his country to abandon certain reprehensible practices. He was as much at fault as anyone else, and he said so. Consequently, the need for his opponents to defend themselves would be reduced and the way made easier for them to consider moving away from these practices.

Humor: A Valuable Ally in the Midst of Serious Work

A third lesson to learn from Wilberforce is a surprising one, namely, that humor is to be cherished, no matter how serious the work one is involved in. Laughter has been called the best medicine. Sometimes, however, we aren't very good at laughing, whether at ourselves or at the funny things that happen around us like a slip of the tongue or the funny things that children say. We miss the humor in these incidents because we're not attuned to and watching for it. We have no funny bone.

Like anything else, practice in this area makes perfect, which is why some people seem to see humor everywhere. They have a comical perspective and entertaining comment on most everything that happens to them, and they are a breath of fresh air at any gathering.

But can we really maintain a humorous outlook when the work we are engaged in is deadly serious? Should we do so? As difficult as it may be for some to see how Wilberforce could laugh, knowing the repugnant facts he knew about the slave trade and other injustices in his culture, he maintained a powerful wit and sense of humor throughout his lifetime. He was known to many as the funniest member in the entire House of Commons. Those sitting near him were often brought to tears of laughter from his comments during the speeches of others.

How could anyone be this funny knowing slaves were being rounded up, brutalized and killed, children were being treated inhumanely in the country's underground mines, and many British citizens were being held in prisons by ruthless debtor laws? Isn't such laughter cruel and insensitive, the sign of a hardened heart? In Wilberforce's case, nothing could be further from the truth. Such descriptions simply didn't fit him. At the same time as he was demonstrating such joviality, he was also giving his energy, time, skills, wealth and, in the end, his very life to fighting these shameful practices. Cruel and insensitive he was not. There had to be some other explanation for his humor and wit.

HUMOR IS TO BE CHERISHED.

Two facts may help us understand how this was possible for Wilberforce—and is for us as well. First, we should at the very least realize that maintaining a dour, gloomy outlook does nothing to make us more effective in bringing about cultural change. It neither makes our message more appealing nor does it make life one iota better for those for whom we are trying to effect change. In fact, the opposite is usually true. The more energetic and positive we come across, the more likely people will be to give us a hearing.

Second, let's not forget that working against shameful and cruel practices such as Wilberforce was opposing is fundamentally positive work. This is a truth often missed because of how negative it seems to be working *against* anything, particularly issues like slavery or child labor or debtor laws. We would rather be fighting *for* than *against* something. The reality, however, is that opposing unjust and cruel practices is simply part of standing up *for* deeper positive principles and values that benefit our fellow citizens but which are being violated by unjust practices. If we truly stand for something, we have no choice but also to oppose that which violates what we stand for.

For Wilberforce, slavery was abhorrent because it violated both the inherent dignity of humanity and the freedom that all humans deserve to make life's big choices for themselves. These are positive principles worth fighting for and celebrating, both in Wilberforce's time and in ours. It makes sense for people who are defending something this positive and beneficial to do so joyfully, with gusto and, yes, to laugh while they do it.

It would be a worthwhile exercise for all of us to examine the practices or policies we oppose and to identify the deeper, positive principles and truths that lie behind our opposition and are violated by the policies. Once we have identified these underlying principles, our efforts can be aimed with greater precision and gusto at upholding and celebrating them. Why not laugh or at least smile as we do so?

Arguments Have Their Limitations

We dare not miss the fourth lesson from Wilberforce since it directly affects how effective we are in making our case to the world. We all have probably had the experience of watching someone laugh off a particular argument or line of reasoning we found to be downright persuasive with the simple comment, "I just don't find that convincing." We shake our heads when we hear that. How can this be? Didn't they hear us properly? Weren't we clear in stating our case? What went wrong? If the argument was convincing to us, why wasn't it equally convincing to everybody else?

Whatever else an experience like that may do to us, it points out the fact that arguments have their limitations, and if we're not aware of them, it will lead to confusion and frustration. As we saw earlier, some people tend to underestimate the value of arguments and actually wonder whether we ought to abandon their use altogether. But it's also possible for us to overestimate their power to persuade others. We may expect that if our position is sound and well stated, others should, and eventually will, be convinced by it; all we need to do is put together our case well and we'll begin to see others agree with us. Perhaps we need a reality check here.

Most everything has limitations: your family car, your personal computer, your body, your mind, your money and everything else you own. For something to have limitations does not mean it is deficient or flawed. It isn't a bad thing at all. But we make a mistake when we ignore the limitations things have and expect them to perform beyond what they are able or designed to do.

Arguments are no different. They too have their limitations. But in their case, the limitations are not necessarily due to any flaw in the arguments themselves. Rather, limitations exist, at least some of the time, because of their connection to human beings. Even the best argument is directed toward some person or group of people. We human beings are not computers or slot machines; we can't plug in an argument and expect a changed mind to come out. We are complex personalities. We have preferences, background experiences, biases, perspectives, hopes and aims, all of which cause us to see things differently than others, to weigh data and evidence differently than others, and to be convinced by different things than others are. In fact, if we're honest we'll even admit that at times we *want* certain things to be true and others to be false. Desires like these have a way of complicating what even the most rigorous argument can do, and few people have been as clear in admitting this last fact as the atheist philosopher Thomas Nagel, who wrote his now famous and astoundingly honest words:

> I speak from experience, being strongly subject to this fear [of religion] myself; some of the most intelligent and well-informed people I know are religious believers. It isn't just that I don't believe in God and, naturally, hope that I'm right in my belief. It's that I hope there is no God! I don't want there to be a God; I don't want a universe to be like that.[7]

The point we dare not miss here is that it is one thing to present a sound argument, quite another to see someone actually persuaded by it. And if our goal is to persuade, we may have to get more creative and do more work than we first thought. Clear logic and compelling argumentation may turn out to be foundational, even indispensable, but nowhere near sufficient for the task when standing alone.

This reality about argumentation is sometimes forgotten, but not by Wilberforce. He appeared to recognize more than most that the soundness of an argument or point of view is no guarantee that either will win the day. Far from it. The presence of child labor and slavery were ample evidence of that. Others had argued against them, all without success.

---

[7]Thomas Nagel, *The Last Word* (New York: Oxford University Press, 1997), p. 130.

What then did he do? His goal was not simply to give gripping or entertaining speeches. It was to convince his fellow citizens to change entrenched national social and economic policies from which they were reaping enormous benefits. Did he concede that arguments have limited power and give up on them altogether? Quite the opposite. In Wilberforce's mind, arguments had to be made again and again, in different ways and through different means, in the House of Commons and outside it, to the elites of society and to the masses, through speeches and pamphlets. He used every means he could, and in the end his message prevailed.

In other words he appeared to recognize that while arguments have limitations, they are not powerless. If someone wasn't convinced by a sound argument, maybe they could be persuaded when the argument was framed differently or communicated through a different vehicle or supported by a different set of relevant facts or accompanied by a visual demonstration. We likewise would do well to exercise tenacity and creativity both in the ways we make our cases and the means we use to get them across. It is a long-distance run, not a 100-meter dash.

SOCIAL JUSTICE: AN INCREMENTAL PROCESS

The fifth lesson to learn from William Wilberforce may be the hardest of all for some people. It is that achieving social justice is a slow and incremental process. The often plodding, step-by-step nature of Wilberforce's strategy comes as a bitter pill to some social activists today. In their zeal to achieve a specific goal, whether banning abortion on demand, eliminating poverty or improving labor laws, some today operate with an "all or nothing" mentality. Anything less than accomplishing one's full goal all at once is viewed as an unacceptable compromise, as giving tacit approval to an unjust practice.

Not Wilberforce. Though his ultimate goal was clearly to abolish slavery in the British Empire, it quickly became clear that immediate emancipation was neither possible nor practical. He began to realize the power of incremental progress.[8] If the slave *trade* could be done away

---

[8]For a discussion on Wilberforce's use of an incremental strategy, see Pollock, *Wilberforce,* pp. 142-43; and Lean, *God's Politician,* pp. 49-61.

with, he reasoned, the cruelties of the trade itself would end and the supply of slaves would be cut off. It was hoped this would force slave owners to treat their present slaves better because they would be irreplaceable. So for a time he moved to end the slave *trade*.[9]

At one point he supported a one-year experimental bill, introduced by a friend, to regulate the number of slaves that could be transported on each ship.[10] Often the ships used weren't designed for human cargo and as many slaves as possible were crammed in. In one instance, 340 slaves out of a cargo of 540 died on a short voyage.[11] If slavery couldn't be stopped immediately, at least slaves could be treated more humanely while it lasted. The bill passed when members of Parliament visited a slave ship for themselves and saw the inhumane conditions in which slaves were transported.

At another time Wilberforce voted for a bill (The Registry of Slaves Bill) requiring plantation owners to register all slaves kept on each island. His thinking was that once the exact number of slaves was recorded no slave owner could add to his slave gangs from blacks smuggled in by slave traders defying the abolition laws. Thus a register would stifle smuggling, force owners to treat their slaves properly and thus prepare slaves to become a "free peasantry."[12] On a different occasion, an order was given limiting the whipping of slaves.

The value of achieving incremental success was at least twofold: First, even if slavery was never to be abolished, at least life would become more tolerable for slaves. Second, and more powerfully, once Wilberforce's opponents had voted for better treatment for slaves, they had implicitly stepped onto the slippery slope that could end only in total abolition. If it was good to limit the whipping of slaves or to create more humane conditions for them on the ships, it must be because they had more worth and dignity than animals. If they didn't, why vote for these more humane conditions? But if the slaves did have more worth than an-

---

[9]Lean, *God's Politician*, pp. 49-50.
[10]Pollock, *Wilberforce*, p. 144.
[11]Ibid., pp. 251-52.
[12]Ibid., pp. 249-50.

imals, how could supporters of the slave trade continue to condone slavery at all? By voting for certain bills, Wilberforce's opponents had tacitly agreed to certain principles that Wilberforce could then use to argue for still better treatment of slaves, and ultimately for abolition. These incremental successes had provided the basis for ending the slave trade.[13]

It's worth noting that others have used this incremental approach with great effectiveness in a variety of issues. Its use is not limited to promoting any particular set of social or moral viewpoints. It's a strategy, pure and simple, and like most strategies, it can be employed to bring about change in more than one direction.

A few decades ago when abortion was uncommon and largely illegal, proponents of it argued that it ought to be made available as a special measure for women whose physical health was threatened by a pregnancy. It wasn't difficult to press this point home by pointing to expectant mothers, real people, whose health or very lives appeared to be at risk from their pregnancies. High-risk pregnancies are a fact of life.

This line of reasoning seemed hard to refute because how could anyone argue that the life of an unborn child was *more valuable* than the life of its mother if a choice had to be made between the two? At the very least, this grim choice must be in the hands of the mother whose very life stood to be affected by it, not the government, and so abortion must be available to these mothers.

Once abortion was granted for that reason, however, proponents extended their argument to include *mental* health. If *physical* health should be protected, why not *mental* health as well? Is a woman's *body* important but not her *mind*, as one person put it to me a number of years ago? And so eventually abortion became legally available for this reason as well.

But, of course, mental health is a broader, more ambiguous concept than physical health, one which gave physicians greater freedom to signify that pregnancies were causing undue stress or in some way threatening the mental or emotional well-being of women who sought abortions. The number of abortions began to rise, and abortion came

---

[13]Ibid., pp. 87-89.

to be increasingly accepted throughout society.

This wider acceptance allowed pro-choice advocates to again broaden their argument and simply contend that the right to an abortion was part of women's reproductive rights. Cases of rape and incest were highlighted as especially important, but in the end the claim was that no one should be able to tell a woman she had to carry any pregnancy to full term. The choice either to have a baby or not should be a woman's choice and no one else's. Over time anti-abortion legislation came to be viewed as anti-women legislation because it violated a woman's reproductive rights.[14]

However we may feel about the success of those fighting this battle, what is clear is that the incremental strategy proved to be highly effective, just as it was for Wilberforce. It is effective because it capitalizes on two important insights. The first is that people are usually far more willing to make small changes in social policy than large ones. The larger and more dramatic the change, the more it moves us beyond what we are familiar or comfortable with. Most of us find it easier to move to something we know and understand than to something we don't.

A subtle but unmistakable fear of the unknown is why, in common parlance, we have expressions like, "better the devil you know than the one you don't." People can often be convinced to go along with a change by being told that it won't really be that different from what they are doing now. And, in fact, often when a person resists a particular change, he or she will argue that the wished-for change is not small at all but is really significant and will outline ways it does represent serious change. The size of the change itself becomes an argument against it. The incremental strategy recognizes this human impulse and breaks large changes into small steps.

The second insight is really an extension of the first. It is that governments are often like big ships, slow to change course. Institutions, traditions and accepted ways of doing things become established and are not easily set aside. This is not a bad thing since it creates a sense of stability

---

[14]For an overview of the history of abortion in America, including arguments and strategies employed, see former United States Surgeon General C. Everett Koop's book *The Right to Live; The Right to Die* (Wheaton, Ill.: Tyndale House, 1976), esp. pp. 32-50.

and security in any society. A nation in which foundational changes to established institutions and policies happen easily and often would be a fearful nation to live in.

But this stability also has important implications for anyone seeking to bring about change in society. It means that often the only way to bring about a large change is to break it down into several baby steps.

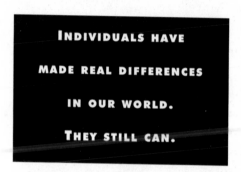

INDIVIDUALS HAVE

MADE REAL DIFFERENCES

IN OUR WORLD.

THEY STILL CAN.

These are valuable insights this incremental strategy recognizes.

Why then do some people continue to express serious doubts about this approach? What problem could anyone have with an incremental strategy that is this insightful and successful in bringing about change? The problem, as earnestly expressed from time to time, is that this approach involves voting for or otherwise supporting social policies that allow immoral practices to continue. For Wilberforce, voting for policies that banned the whipping of slaves or that called for slaves to be registered or transported in more humane conditions meant slavery could continue. In fact, technically, it meant that he was voting *for slavery* so long as these conditions were met. Doesn't this mean he was giving tacit approval to slavery? Doesn't it mean we are doing the same if we use an incremental strategy when working against an unjust social policy today? Aren't we compromising our own convictions? How can we sleep at night or live with our consciences when we are supporting unjust practices? This genuine concern is expressed by highly principled people, and we should not disregard it.

I know of one prominent Christian politician who voted in favor of legislation that would place tighter restrictions on the practice of abortion than presently exists but still permits abortions to occur for reasons many in the pro-life community disagree with. As much as this member, and others in the government with pro-life convictions, would have preferred still tighter restrictions, it was not possible to gain sufficient support for them in the governing cabinet or caucus. This was the best that could be done given the present mood. Upon returning to his conservative constituency, he was roundly and loudly criticized by his supporters for allegedly compromising his convictions and settling for something less than the best.[15]

Another candidate for national office who also had strong pro-life convictions made it clear to those near him that if elected he could never vote for legislation that allowed abortion for anything other than the most severe reasons. Anything else would be an unacceptable compromise. It would mean his vote allowed this practice to continue, and he simply could not live with that.[16]

What should we say about this fear? Does it point to a serious problem with an incremental strategy? Does it mean that, for all its insights and successes, a principled person has no choice but to reject it on pain of acting in an unprincipled manner?

In deciding this question we must be careful to avoid a subtle and easy mistake, namely, that of comparing two options of which only one is a real live alternative and the other is entirely unattainable, and then acting as though we can decide which is the best between these two. Those who voice this concern over using an incremental strategy make the mistake of comparing a proposed policy change (which is a step in the right direction but does not go as far as they believe it ought to) with some other perfect but unattainable policy, and then asking which of those two they prefer. That is an easy question, but it is the wrong one since only one of these options is attainable and the other is not. This is not dealing with reality, and it does nothing to improve the plight of those we are trying to help or protect.

Obviously, Wilberforce would have preferred an outright ban on sla-

[15]I refer here to the honorable Jake Epp, Canada's minister of health during the 1980s in the Conservative government led by Prime Minister Brian Mulroney. The abortion bill I mention here was eventually killed in Canada's senate, and so it was never enacted into law.
[16]This reference is to a candidate for the Progressive Conservative party of Canada in the province of Ontario in the federal election of 1997. His son, one of my students, discussed this issue with me at the time and told me of his father's convictions in this regard.

very to policies that merely made life better for slaves, but a ban was not possible at that time and, therefore, was not a real option for him to consider. When it came to voting for or against improved conditions on the slave ships, the real choice before him was between *slavery with inhumane transport conditions* and *slavery with somewhat improved conditions.* And we have to ask, given those two genuine options, what principle is there that would require we vote for the former, especially when voting for the latter would also have the additional benefit of creating the basis for future arguments against the institution of slavery itself?

Wilberforce and others taught us the value of an incremental strategy, and we would do well to emulate them and even perfect this strategy further in working for social justice today.

GIFTS TO THE WORLD

The lives of William Wilberforce and others like him have been a profound benefit to the world. We are different because they were here. These social activists were paragons of perseverance in the struggle for justice, not for themselves but for others. They fought for what they knew was right and were not deterred by opposition. They developed strategies for change and at all times were guided by unshakable moral truths. At the end of the day they mastered the art of engaging the people of their culture, persuading them to change course.

One thing is clear: opposition will always exist for anyone, any time, who takes up the call to change his or her culture morally and socially. One lesson, however, rings loud and clear: individuals have made real differences in our world. They still can.